LINCOLN'S MORAL VISION

LINCOLN'S MORAL VISION

The Second Inaugural Address

James Tackach

UNIVERSITY PRESS OF MISSISSIPPI   JACKSON

www.upress.state.ms.us

Copyright © 2002 by University Press of Mississippi

All rights reserved

Manufactured in the United States of America

10 09 08 07 06 05 04 03 02   4 3 2 1

∞

Library of Congress Cataloging-in-Publication Data

Tackach, James.
    Lincoln's moral vision : the second inaugural address / James Tackach.
        p.   cm.
    Includes index.
        ISBN 1-57806-495-3 (cloth : alk. paper)
        1. Lincoln, Abraham, 1809–1865—Inauguration, 1865.   2. Lincoln,
    Abraham, 1809–1865—Political and social views. 3. United States—
    Politics and government—1861–1865.   4. United States—Moral
    conditions.   5. Presidents—United States—Inaugural addresses.
    6. Speeches, addresses, etc., American—History and criticism.
    I. Title.

    E457.94 1865e
    973.7'092—dc21   2002002032

British Library Cataloging-in-Publication Data available

To my mother, Loretta M. Tackach,
who first revealed to me the beauty of books

"It is a truth which I thought needed to be told."

—ABRAHAM LINCOLN
*commenting on his Second Inaugural Address
in a letter to Thurlow Weed, March 15, 1865*

CONTENTS

ACKNOWLEDGMENTS

No author works alone. All books are team efforts, and I was fortunate to have the University Press of Mississippi editing team working with me on the manuscript that became this book. I am especially grateful to editor-in-chief Craig W. Gill for accepting my manuscript, even though a book on Abraham Lincoln's Second Inaugural Address was scheduled for publication several months before this book could reach the bookstores. I am also grateful to Robert Burchfield for his careful copyediting of my manuscript—every one of his suggestions improved the text—and to the staff at the University Press of Mississippi who helped to direct copies of this book into bookstores and on-line catalogs. These people had me convinced that my book was the only one they were publishing this year.

I also wish to acknowledge the cooperation of Michael Schuldiner, editor of *Studies in Puritan American Spirituality*. A streamlined version of Chapter 6 of this text appears in the 2002 edition of that journal.

Finally, I offer a special thanks to my colleagues and students, past and present, at Roger Williams University. These folks have inspired all of my best ideas.

INTRODUCTION

In an article published on the op-ed page of the *New York Times* in 1998, Thomas Geoghegan lamented that Americans remember so little of Abraham Lincoln's Second Inaugural Address, that the only passage of this great speech residing in our collective memories is the last paragraph, the beautiful sentence commencing "With malice toward none; with charity for all." Geoghegan, perhaps urging some scholar to accept the assignment, suggests that the Second Inaugural "is worth a book as good as the one Garry Wills wrote on the Gettysburg Address"—a speech that remains fresh in the minds of many Americans, perhaps because schoolchildren are still required to commit it to memory, perhaps because fine scholars like Wills remain attracted to it.[1]

Indeed, the Gettysburg Address has been the subject of at least five books.[2] Its centennial was marked with academic conferences and published papers by important Lincoln scholars who, at the start of the twenty-first century, continue to explore Lincoln's dedicatory remarks at Gettysburg cemetery. By comparison, the Second Inaugural Address, which Wills calls "the only speech worthy to stand with" Lincoln's Gettysburg declaration, has received scant attention.[3] Twenty years ago, William Lee Miller observed that the Second Inaugural "as a whole has not often received the full portal-to-portal examination accorded that more famous address by Lincoln, or the Declaration of Independence, or the Preamble to the Constitution (not to mention, at the hands of lawyers, the Constitution itself)."[4] Despite the great scholarly output on Lincoln during the past two decades, Miller's assertion remains valid. To Geoghegan's apparent dismay, no book-length study of Lincoln's Second Inaugural Address was in print at the turn of the twenty-first century. That is unfortunate because the 701-word Second Inaugural, delivered sixteen months after Lincoln's remarks at Gettysburg and only forty-two days before his death, is, in many ways, the more revealing, if not the more stylistically pleasing, speech—more revealing because the later speech discloses Lincoln's thinking, at the end of his life, on key issues with which he had grappled throughout his long political career: slavery and race, the meaning of nationhood, the purpose of government, the role of God in the universe.

Wills's brilliant book on the Gettysburg Address presents a close analysis of Lincoln's words, re-creates Lincoln's composition process, and discusses the special occasion for which the speech was delivered—the dedication of a military cemetery at the time of a great civil war during America's Romantic Age. This study of Lincoln's Second Inaugural Address attempts a similar feat; it closely analyzes Lincoln's words of March 4, 1865, and the context in which he spoke them—a presidential inauguration ceremony near the end of a civil war that already had cost the opposing sides more than six hundred thousand lives and would completely transform their nation. But because the Second Inaugural is, in a sense, a speech of culmination, a major address delivered by Lincoln to the American people very close to the end of his life, this study of that speech devotes considerable space to an examination of the key issues explored in it as they unfolded in Lincoln's mind during his thirty-year political career.

To that end, this study develops four major premises. First, the Abraham Lincoln portrayed here is neither Satan nor saint nor prophet; he is neither the consummate politician whose every word and action are prompted by political expediency nor an unregenerate racist, as suggested by some revisionist scholars of the late twentieth century. The Lincoln presented in this study is a mere mortal, shaped by the attitudes of his time and place, who lived what Plato's Socrates would have called the examined life and who, in doing so, grappled in a moving way with the key issues of his day and revealed his deliberations on these issues to his countrymen and countrywomen in some of the most poignant prose delivered by an American president.[5] The Lincoln of this study is a complex man with a remarkable mind who defies the easy categorization attempted by some who have written about Lincoln.

The view that Lincoln is Satan incarnate developed during his lifetime. To Southerners, Lincoln was a tyrant who brought a devastating war upon the South's plantation society. At best, Lincoln was a nineteenth-century George III, stifling the South's impulse toward independence. John Wilkes Booth spoke for millions of Southerners when he referred to Lincoln as a blackguard and a Caesar who laid waste to the entire South. Throughout the South during and after the Civil War, Lincoln's reputation remained virtually unchanged. This view of Lincoln survived into the twentieth century, supported, strangely enough, by, among others, two Northern men of letters, Edgar Lee Masters and Edmund Wilson. Masters's 1931 study, *Lincoln the Man*, would have provided good reading for Booth. For Masters, Lincoln was a cold-hearted, opportunistic politician who waged a cruel and illegal war upon the South and, in the process, crushed the noble principles of democratic government.[6] Masters was attempting to provide, perhaps, a corrective to the heroic image of Lincoln portrayed in Carl Sandburg's popular biography, whose first two volumes, titled *Abraham Lincoln: The Prairie Years*, appeared in 1926.[7]

Wilson is only somewhat less harsh than Masters. In *Patriotic Gore*, his study of the American writers of the Civil War, Wilson challenges the prevailing view of Lincoln that developed during the twentieth century—that Lincoln was a man of the people who waged a war to free the slaves and thereby set the United States on a proper moral course so that the nation might achieve the worthy goals put forth by the "Founding Fathers" in the great national documents of the eighteenth century. According to Wilson, "There has undoubtedly been written about him [Lincoln] more romantic and sentimental rubbish than about any other American figure, with the possible exception of Edgar Allan Poe." Wilson lumps Lincoln with Otto von Bismarck and Vladimir Ilyich Lenin, each of whom "became an uncompromising dictator" while ruthlessly unifying his country and thereby turning it into a great power. Wilson compares Lincoln's war against the South in 1865 to the Soviet Union's subjugation of the rebellion in Hungary in 1956. For Wilson, Lincoln's war was no noble cause; it had little to do with freeing the slaves or upholding the principles of democratic government. The North's suppression of the Confederacy was simply "the competition for power for its own sake."[8]

Such a view of Lincoln and his era, however, is open to the charge of reductionism. To Southerners, Lincoln was, and perhaps remains, a tyrant; his war surely destroyed the South's plantation society. But to reduce Lincoln to the role of ruthless conquistador and his war to a mere campaign for political subjection requires one to nullify as "patriotic gore" most of Lincoln's words and to ignore the deep divisions in American society caused by the slavery issue in the mid-nineteenth century. For many Northerners, the Civil War was indeed a moral crusade to rid the land of slavery or a conflict to test the survivability of democratic government. And Lincoln himself, who initially considered the war in political terms—a war of rebellion against his authority as president—eventually saw the conflict in moral and religious terms—as God's punishment to both the North and South for the sin of slavery.

As the South condemned Lincoln to the lower circles of hell, the North canonized him, a process that began at the time of his death. During the dark days following Lincoln's assassination, ministers throughout the North extolled Lincoln as a redeemer who freed the nation of slavery and who, on Good Friday, gave his life so that the nation's sins may be forgiven. To the freed slaves, Lincoln became a Moses or Father Abraham, a messiah who led a downtrodden people from bondage to the promised land of freedom. Perhaps, as Alfred Kazin suggests, "The triumphant North needed proof of its saintliness, and found it in the consecration of Abraham Lincoln."[9] And this view of Lincoln survived into the twentieth century. In 1922, the United States government dedicated, on Washington, D.C.'s most prominent mall, an Athenian temple to honor the nation's mid-nineteenth-century god. Behind the impressive Doric columns of the Lincoln Memorial the prophet-president sits like a god upon a heavenly throne. Visitors worship at his feet.

Some late-twentieth-century Lincoln scholars still portray Lincoln in godly terms. William Wolf compares Lincoln to the seers of ancient Israel, asserting that "Lincoln stands among God's latter-day prophets."[10] Writing in celebration of the one hundredth anniversary of the Gettysburg Address, the novelist John Dos Passos called Lincoln "the care-worn national prophet who spoke at Gettysburg."[11] This Lincoln preached with the voice of a biblical prophet to God's newly chosen people, who had strayed from their national goal of keeping democracy alive in the world. By waging a war to defend democratic government and by freeing the slaves—while invoking the Lord to justify his actions—Lincoln advanced God's work on earth. Lincoln's speeches and writings are sacred texts, a national scripture.

But this view of Lincoln ignores the fact that he was, in the words of one recent Lincoln biographer, "a typical Victorian doubter" who became a devout believer out of exasperation—as a result of his inability to understand why such a terrible war had come to his country.[12] He carried no tablets from God. He never claimed to hold God's truth; in his most moving religious statements, he presents himself as an uncertain mortal struggling to make sense of things he could barely understand. Unlike Plato's Socrates, Lincoln mentioned no private conferences with God. As Elton Trueblood asserts, "He was no flaming prophet like John the Baptist."[13] Reinhold Niebuhr calls Lincoln "not a moral prophet . . . but a responsible statesman."[14] Prophets lead people. Lincoln stated, in an April 1864 letter, "I claim not to have controlled events, but confess plainly that events have controlled me."[15] He was a mere mortal, a Victorian skeptic, eventually brought to God by personal and national tragedies, who made great efforts to determine God's will.

Perhaps as a reaction against this saintly view of Lincoln, Richard Hofstadter, in an influential essay published in 1948, presented Lincoln as "thoroughly and completely the politician, by preference and by training." Hofstadter's Lincoln was unconcerned with the slavery issue until 1854, and he eventually engaged in the prewar slavery debate for political rather than moral reasons: "Only after the Kansas-Nebraska Act breathed political life into the slavery issue did he seize upon it as a subject for agitation; only then did he attack it openly. His attitude was based on justice tempered by expediency—or perhaps more accurately, expediency tempered by justice."[16]

Few would argue that Lincoln was not a skillful politician. The manner in which he worked to secure his nomination at the Republican presidential convention in 1860, the skill with which he handled crises in his cabinet during his presidency, the diplomacy that he showed in dealing with Great Britain during the Civil War—all attest to this shrewd frontier lawyer's political proficiency. But he was not an example of the elected official motivated solely by political ambitions; public opinion polls did not fix Lincoln's political positions. To the contrary, Lincoln, throughout his career, displayed a willingness to take unpopular political stances that jeopardized his own standing with voters. For example, early in his public career, in late 1847, when he served in the House of Representatives, Lincoln stated his opposition to the Mexican War. In the debates for the 1858 Illinois Senate seat, Stephen Douglas hammered Lincoln for taking that position. "When the Mexican war [was] being waged, and the American army was surrounded by the enemy in Mexico, he thought that war was unconstitutional, unnecessary, and unjust," Douglas asserted during the debate at Alton, Illinois (3:319). Lincoln earned the derisive nickname "Spotty" because he had demanded to know the spot on United States soil where Mexican troops had attacked the United States Army. Later, in the summer and fall of 1862, Lincoln, as president, called for a military draft, suspended the writ of habeas corpus, and announced the Preliminary Emancipation Proclamation—unpopular decisions that cost the Republican Party thirty seats in the House of Representatives in the November elections. Lincoln continued the war effort through the summer and fall of 1864, even though he sensed that staying the course might result in his defeat on election day. On August 23, 1864, less than three months before the 1864 presidential election, Lincoln wrote a Memorandum Concerning His Probable Failure of Re-election, in which he stated that "it seems exceedingly probable that this Administration will not be re-elected" (7:514).

Hofstadter argues that Lincoln seized upon the passage of the 1854 Kansas-Nebraska Act as an issue to revitalize his own moribund political career, that he opposed its passage for political reasons rather than in moral outrage over the possible spread of slavery into the United States territories. It is true that Lincoln reentered the political fray after Douglas shepherded the Kansas-Nebraska Act and the concept of popular sovereignty through Congress, but Lincoln's concern over the prospect of slavery spreading to the territories, expressed in dozens of speeches and writings between 1854 and 1860, rings genuine. And Lincoln was not the only Northerner to express his misgivings about Douglas's 1854 legislation. "Lincoln's reaction [to the Kansas-Nebraska Act] typifies the awakening of many sober-minded men in the North," states Don E. Fehrenbacher. "Always opposed in principle to the institution of slavery, he had not hitherto enlisted actively in the crusade against it."[17] Allen C. Guelzo concurs with Hofstadter that Lincoln saw "the turmoil over the Kansas-Nebraska bill as an opportunity for his own personal advancement." But Guelzo suggests that Lincoln's motivation for speaking out on the Kansas-Nebraska legislation was more than political: "But Lincoln was motivated by infinitely more than just the bubble opportunities provided by the Kansas-Nebraska uproar. The whole bill—from the establishment of popular sovereignty to the dismantling of the Missouri Compromise—struck at the very heart of Lincoln's Whiggish complacency about slavery."[18]

Compare Lincoln's reaction to the Kansas-Nebraska Act to Harriet Beecher Stowe's and Henry David Thoreau's reaction to the Fugitive Slave Law. Stowe, who was raised in an abolitionist family and married an abolitionist, always believed slavery to be immoral, but she did not feel outraged enough about the institution to speak out against it in public until the passage of the Fugitive Slave Law in 1850. Shortly after the passage of that legislation (which was part of the Compromise of 1850), Stowe wrote to Gamaliel Bailey, editor of the antislavery *National Era*, of her reaction to the bill: "Up to this year I have always felt that I had no particular call to meddle with this subject [slavery], and I dreaded to expose my own mind to the full force of its exciting power. But I feel now that the time is come when even a woman or a child who can speak a word for freedom and humanity is bound to speak. . . . I hope every woman who can write will not be silent."[19] In that same letter, Stowe described a series of sketches that she was writing about slavery—sketches that would become the greatest piece of antebellum antislavery literature, *Uncle Tom's Cabin*.

Thoreau was similarly energized by the passage of the Fugitive Slave Law. In "Civil Disobedience," composed a year before the passage of the law, Thoreau announced his divorce from the state of Massachusetts; he requested not to be involved with the state's affairs, and he hoped that the state would not disturb him in any way. In July 1854, Thoreau published, in William Lloyd Garrison's antislavery newspaper, the *Liberator*, "Slavery in Massachusetts" in reaction to the arrest of Anthony Burns, a refugee slave living in Massachusetts. In that address, Thoreau expressed his outrage over the passage of the Fugitive Slave Law, a law that "rises not to the level of the head or the reason; its natural habitat is in the dirt." Thoreau also announced that he was no longer the disinterested citizen described in "Civil Disobedience": "I had never respected the Government near to which I had lived, but I had foolishly thought that I might manage to live here, minding my private affairs, and forget it." But, he adds, "It is not an era of repose. We have used up all our inherited freedom. If we would save our lives, we must fight for them."[20] Thereafter, Thoreau became active in the antislavery movement.

If the Fugitive Slave Law could energize Thoreau and Stowe, surely the passage of the Kansas-Nebraska Act could roust Lincoln from his complacency about slavery. Hofstadter's argument that Lincoln became engaged in the national debate over slavery for purely political reasons fails to consider the possibility that people can be changed, can be morally and politically energized by world or national events. Fehrenbacher writes sensibly when he states, "Between hero worship and cynicism there is a middle view which recognizes in Lincoln both the man of deep moral conviction and the practical, aspiring politician."[21]

More devastating than Hofstadter's critique of Lincoln was an attack waged against him during the late 1960s by African American scholars, who saw in Lincoln a spokesman for white supremacy. To support their claims, these scholars point to Lincoln's reticence to embrace the abolitionist cause, his advocacy for plans to colonize African Americans in Africa and South America, his acceptance of the Fugitive Slave Law, and his statements about the inferiority of blacks during his 1858 debates with Stephen Douglas and elsewhere. In an influential article that appeared in *Ebony* magazine in 1968, Lerone Bennett Jr. asserts that "the real Lincoln was a tragically flawed figure who shared the racial prejudices of most of his white contemporaries."[22] Like Bennett, Julius Lester, in a 1968 book titled *Look Out, Whitey! Black Power's Gon' Get Your Mama!*, faults President Lincoln for taking two years to issue the Emancipation Proclamation: "Blacks have no reason to feel grateful to Abraham Lincoln. How come it took him two whole years to free the slaves? His pen was sitting on his desk the whole time."[23]

This view of Lincoln put forth by African American activist scholars like Bennett and Lester has also been embraced by twenty-first-century white supremacists, who find in Lincoln support for their racist positions. A recent article in the *New York Times* reports that the website of a contemporary white supremacist organization offers an image of a lynched black man with the alleged words of Lincoln beneath: "I can conceive of no greater calamity than the assimilation of the Negro into our social and political life as an equal."[24]

Commenting upon attempts to portray Lincoln as a white supremacist or a racist, Elton Trueblood flatly states, "This effort does not merit much attention."[25] The Civil War scholar James M. McPherson, in reviewing Bennett's recent book on Lincoln, *Forced into Glory: Abraham Lincoln's White Dream*, disagrees, stating that Bennett's harsh critique of Lincoln "must be taken seriously."[26] Nonetheless, McPherson identifies weaknesses in Bennett's argument that can be leveled against other scholars who maintain that Lincoln was a racist. Their claim often rests on selective evidence taken out of context from Lincoln's early speeches and writings and ignores contradictory evidence. Bennett's argument also fails to consider the opinions of African Americans on Lincoln during his presidency. Although Frederick Douglass and other African American civil rights leaders often sharply criticized Lincoln's policies, claiming that Lincoln moved too slowly on emancipation and on civil rights initiatives, the majority of African Americans greatly admired the sixteenth president, a point made by Benjamin Quarles in his 1962 study, *Lincoln and the Negro*: "Yet the Negroes of his day saw him as a man growing in knowledge and wisdom, and to them he was emancipator, benefactor, friend, and leader." Quarles considers the argument that Lincoln proceeded too slowly with a program for emancipation as "a minority report [that] was not even discussed and died because no one would second it."[27]

Those who place the racist label upon Lincoln also fail to consider his growth and development in the area of civil rights. The enlightened statements about slavery and race made by Lincoln during the final two years of his life perhaps do not negate his earlier troubling assertions about the social and intellectual superiority of the white race, but his remarks about blacks and slavery made after emancipation do suggest an increased sensitivity to racial issues. As Fawn M. Brodie suggests, the argument that Lincoln was a racist is "bolstered by a dexterous selection of early Lincoln statements and by ignoring the steady evolution of Lincoln's attitude toward Negro rights and the massive evidence of his cooperation with men in the radical wing of his party [strong proponents of rights for the freed slave] and they with him." According to Brodie, Lincoln's record "is as certain a march in the direction of Negro freedom as that of Jefferson Davis and Robert E. Lee was away from it."[28]

Brodie's point leads to the second major premise of this study—that Lincoln's attitudes on key issues such as slavery, race, and religion shifted greatly during the Civil War. The guns of Fort Sumter, Shiloh, Antietam, Fredericksburg, Gettysburg, and especially of Milliken's Bend, Port Hudson, and Fort Wagner—battles in which African American soldiers played key roles—shook the foundations of Lincoln's thinking. As Quarles suggests, "War is a rapid educator," and "Lincoln had already shown himself a learner."[29] On December 1, 1862, twenty months into the war—at the end of the year of the massive slaughters at Shiloh, Manassas, and Antietam—Lincoln addressed Congress on the need for a new kind of thinking to deal with the problems facing the nation: "The dogmas of the quiet past, are inadequate to the stormy present," he said (5:537). In this case, Lincoln practiced what he preached. A conservative thinker before the war, a politically and an intellectually cautious man by nature, Lincoln during the war embraced Socrates' advice to lead the examined life, to question his own fixed attitudes on slavery and race, on religion, and on other key issues of his time. The result was significant personal transformation and growth.

Lincoln scholars have identified this capacity for growth, exhibited during his presidency, as one of Lincoln's most remarkable personal traits. David Herbert Donald suggests that Lincoln's "enormous capacity for growth . . . enabled one of the least experienced and most poorly prepared men ever elected to high office to become the greatest American President."[30] Richard N. Current concurs: "The most remarkable thing about him [Lincoln] was his tremendous power of growth. He grew in sympathy, in the breadth of his humaneness, as he grew in other aspects of mind and spirit." According to Current, Lincoln's capacity for growth and change helps reconcile those conflicting images of Lincoln—a racist to some and a champion of civil rights for others: "The one view reflects the position he started from, the other the position he was moving toward. There is confusion regarding particular phases of his Presidential career because nobody knows for sure just what point he had reached at any given moment. But there should be little question as to which way he was going."[31] Similarly, Stephen B. Oates argues that by the end of his life, "In the matter of black political rights, Lincoln was ahead of most members of his party—and far ahead of the vast majority of northern whites at that time."[32] LaWanda Cox sees something "breathtaking" in Lincoln's changing attitude on slavery during his presidency, which she views as "a positive exercise of leadership" and "a ready response to opportunity," not merely "a reluctant accommodation to pressures" from others.[33]

Lincoln's transformation is reflected in his speeches and writings, and that is the third major premise of this study. Some recent Lincoln biographers lament that Lincoln has left us little to determine the workings of his inner life. Mark E. Neely Jr. states that Lincoln "was not given to introspection. Or if he was, he never talked about such subjects or left revealing documents or telltale letters to suggest such a dramatic private or inner life."[34] Similarly, Fehrenbacher remarks that Lincoln "is doubly hard to get at because he did not readily reveal his inner self. He left us no diary or memoirs, and his closest friends called him 'secretive' and 'shut-mouthed.'"[35]

But *The Collected Works of Abraham Lincoln* comprises nine volumes (eight original volumes, plus an index, published in 1953, and a supplemental volume published twenty-one years later). These volumes contain speeches and proclamations, personal and public letters, private meditations and thoughts, even poetry—a collection of documents spanning five decades. Surely these documents provide us with insights into Lincoln's inner landscape. Perhaps in this age of confessional memoirs and tell-all television talk shows we have come to believe that someone must author a salacious autobiography or make a tearful public confession in front of television cameras to reveal his or her own inner feelings. This study rests on the assumption that Lincoln told us much about himself even though he left few writings that would fit the genre of autobiography.

Because of its reliance on Lincoln's own words, this study perhaps better fits the category of literary criticism or literary analysis rather than biography or history.[36] Instead of detailing the life of Lincoln or re-creating his times, this study focuses on one writer's confrontation with the key issues of his time and explores how he resolved these issues in his written works.[37] The biographer and historian would surely make extensive use of Lincoln's own written material as well; indeed, these writings might make up the backbone of any study of Lincoln's life or times. But the biographer or historian would also rely on the statements of Lincoln's contemporaries—what they said he said in private conversations.

When the subject is Lincoln, however, such reminiscences are notoriously unreliable. As Current suggests, "Much of the testimony about Lincoln is priceless. Much of it is trash." The duty of biographers and historians "is to apply the rules of historical evidence to the vast piles of data on Lincoln and his times."[38] Indeed, Lincoln's biographers and historians of his era have had a difficult time separating fact from fiction, and their studies must, to some extent, engage in a debate over which Lincoln sources are reliable. Take, for example, the case of Lincoln's law partner in Springfield, Illinois, William Herndon. Herndon's biography, *Herndon's Lincoln: The True Story of a Great Life*, published in 1889, has become a key source for many Lincoln scholars.[39] Some scholars, however, call Herndon an unreliable narrator, particularly when he records words and actions secondhand rather than relying on his own memories. So a lively debate on Herndon has developed in the Lincoln scholarship. In his biography of Lincoln, Michael Burlingame claims, "I have made extensive use of the Herndon materials."[40] Douglas L. Wilson calls Herndon "an honest and truthful informant."[41] But Charles B. Strozier states that Herndon "created virtually every important myth about Lincoln, and yet his book made him our most important source on the pre-Presidential man." Strozier maintains that when Herndon relied on someone other than himself as a source, "he was usually wrong."[42]

For an example of the hazards facing Lincoln scholars who rely on words attributed to Lincoln by other parties, consider Ward Lamon's comment about Lincoln's evaluation of the Gettysburg Address. According to Lamon, Lincoln's long-time friend and presidential aide, Lincoln, after speaking at Gettysburg, said that his speech "won't scour." Benjamin Barondess assumes that Lincoln actually made that statement.[43] Louis A. Warren states that the "won't scour" expression "sounds much like Lincoln."[44] Indeed it does because Lincoln often used agricultural imagery in his speeches and writings (a plow that will not scour will not plow a field properly). But Garry Wills states that "the myth that Lincoln was disappointed in the result [of his Gettysburg speech]—that he told the unreliable Lamon that his speech, like a bad plow, 'won't scour'—has no basis."[45] Who is correct?

As a work of literary criticism or literary analysis, this study does not have to engage in that kind of debate or assessment of sources. It relies on the words of Lincoln's own speeches and writings, carefully collected by Roy P. Basler. Basler's *Collected Works of Abraham Lincoln* is Lincoln's lifetime literary canon. The materials gathered there provide insight into Lincoln's changing attitudes on the key issues of his day. In the words of Basler, Lincoln's writings and speeches reveal "the slow and constant development of a great mind and personality oriented to the light in the midst of much darkness."[46]

The fourth and final premise of this study is that the Second Inaugural Address signals Lincoln's resolution of these critical issues. Donald suggests that this speech "was a remarkably impersonal address" because Lincoln chose not to use the first-person singular after the speech's opening sentences.[47] But Donald fails to consider that Lincoln, in this oration, touches upon issues with which he had wrestled throughout his political career. On that March day, near the end of the

Civil War and the end of Lincoln's life, Lincoln finally identified the sin of slavery—not the preservation of the Union or the perpetuation of democratic government—as the real cause of his nation's great conflict; he revealed his private conclusions about God's role in the war and in the nation's life; and he opened a pathway on which the nation could travel to reconstruct itself in the aftermath of the great war.

After the Second Inaugural Address, Lincoln would offer only one more public address—a speech on Reconstruction delivered on April 11, 1865, a few days before his assassination. Hence, the Second Inaugural, which Lincoln suggested would "wear as well as—perhaps better than—any thing I have produced" (8:356), represents an endpoint in Lincoln's career, a defining moment of clarification for a man who had struggled to understand the meaning of the crucible through which his country was passing. In his Second Inaugural Address, he had revealed, he later said, "a truth which I thought needed to be told" (8:356). That is not to say that Lincoln had completely resolved the issues that had tested him and his nation for so long. Lincoln lived the examined life; had he lived, he would have continued to struggle with the political and moral dilemmas of the nation as it endeavored to remake itself after a devastating civil war. In the Second Inaugural Address, Lincoln looked both backward and forward—back toward the cause of the nation's crisis and forward toward its full and final resolution.

The first three chapters of this study look backward; they examine three key issues that absorbed Lincoln in his pre-presidential career—slavery, race, and religion. There is, of course, some overlap in these chapters, as Lincoln's racial and religious attitudes shaped his attitude on slavery. Chapters 4 and 5 explore how, during the crucible of war, Lincoln's attitude on these issues shifted in a profound way; how he reevaluated his thinking on slavery, race, and religion; and how his conclusions were reshaped by the great conflict that shook his nation, particularly how Lincoln's positions shifted after 1863, when he emancipated the slaves in the rebellious Southern states and the Union army began to recruit and enlist black soldiers. Chapter 6 focuses closely on the Second Inaugural Address, demonstrating how that speech presents his resolution of these three key issues as well as his thinking on other issues facing the nation at the war's end. The final chapter, an epilogue, speculates on how Lincoln might have confronted the problems facing the country during the postwar years.

Why is this study of Lincoln's Second Inaugural Address necessary after two remarkably impressive decades of Lincoln scholarship? Why have Lincoln scholars devoted so little attention to Lincoln's most revealing speech? Even the best Lincoln scholarship has overlooked or downplayed the Second Inaugural. Donald's long, award-winning biography of Lincoln, for example, devotes only a few pages to the Second Inaugural Address, and Neely's *Last Best Hope on Earth: Abraham Lincoln and the Promise of America* dismisses the Second Inaugural Address as "a less characteristic speech in that it sounded more like a sermon than a secular political appeal."[48] But perhaps Neely's comment might explain, in part, why Lincoln's last great speech escaped book-length analysis for so long. Lincoln's Second Inaugural Address does read like a sermon, as Neely suggests. Perhaps it is too overtly religious for a secular age, an age during which Americans prefer to see religious and political rhetoric living separate lives. Or perhaps the moral relativists and other influential contemporary thinkers of the late twentieth century have found Lincoln's words of March 4, 1865, largely irrelevant at the turn of the twenty-first century. Lincoln's Second Inaugural Address argues for the existence of universal evil—offenses committed by an entire nation that a just God would deem necessary to punish severely. These ideas are not universally embraced in the twenty-first century. What Lincoln said about his Second Inaugural in 1865—"I believe it is not immediately popular" (8:356)—still might hold more than six score years later.

LINCOLN'S MORAL VISION

ONE

Lincoln and Slavery:
"Against the Extension of a Bad Thing"

ON SEPTEMBER 12, 1848, Abraham Lincoln of Illinois made a speech in Worcester, Massachusetts, on behalf of the Whig candidate for the presidency, General Zachary Taylor. The speech covered a variety of issues that were dear to Whigs—the need for a national bank, high tariffs to protect American manufacturers, and government-subsidized "internal improvements" such as the building of roads and the dredging of harbors and rivers. Then Lincoln turned to the issue of slavery. He asserted that "the people of Illinois agreed entirely with the people of Massachusetts on this subject, except perhaps that they did not keep so constantly thinking about it. All agreed that slavery was an evil, but that we were not responsible for it and cannot affect it in the States of the Union where we do not live" (2:3).

Through the 1830s and 1840s Lincoln remained a typical Illinois man. During the 1830s, as a member of the Illinois legislature, Lincoln, as Richard Hofstadter points out, was mainly concerned with moving the state capital from Vandalia to Springfield.[1] During the 1840s, Lincoln remained primarily focused on the items on the Whig Party's probusiness agenda. The list of resolutions adopted at the Illinois Whig convention of June 19, 1844, which Lincoln helped draft, mentions the need for tariffs and a sound currency and a preference for a one-term limit on the tenure of the United States president, but the document says nothing about slavery (1:338–40). The following October, when Lincoln delivered a campaign speech in Rockport, Indiana, for Whig candidates, he devoted most of his time to a discussion of the tariff issue (1:341).

By the mid-1840s, however, the slavery issue was moving to the top of the national agenda. On January 1, 1831, William Lloyd Garrison had published the first issue of his antislavery newspaper, the *Liberator*. An editorial written by Garrison for the paper's first issue boldly asserted his main purpose: "I shall strenuously contend for the immediate enfranchisement of our slave population. . . . I am in earnest—I will not equivocate—I will not excuse—I will not retreat a single inch—AND I WILL BE HEARD."[2] Eight months later, Nat Turner, a Virginia slave, staged his bloody twelve-hour rebellion in Southampton County that resulted in the deaths of some sixty slaveholders and members of their families. An abolitionist pamphlet titled *The Confessions of Nat Turner* was published shortly thereafter, one of the many antislavery texts that would flood the publishing market during the 1830s and 1840s. On November 7, 1837, two hundred proslavery rioters attacked the editorial offices of the *Observer*, an abolitionist newspaper in Alton, Illinois, and murdered its editor, Reverend Elijah P. Lovejoy. During the 1830s and 1840s, an increasing number of runaway slaves from Missouri and Kentucky were crossing the Mississippi and Ohio Rivers to reach the free state of Illinois.

The slavery issue was all over the newspapers in the 1830s and 1840s, but Lincoln said very little about it. With some justification, Lerone Bennett Jr. asserts that throughout the 1830s and 1840s, Lincoln "remained silent and lamentably inactive" on the slavery issue; Bennett views Lincoln as a "cautious politician" and "a man of the fence."[3] Hofstadter maintains that Lincoln, during this period in his life, was not the sort of political maverick who would tackle a controversial issue like slavery, that he was fixed on the standard Whig agenda.[4] Mark E. Neely Jr., perhaps less critical of Lincoln for ignoring the slavery issue for so long, states that Lincoln simply "did not in 1845 think of slavery as a pressing political problem."[5] Lincoln expressed his basic position on slavery in a letter to Williamson Durley, a political supporter, on October 3, 1845. It was "the paramount duty of us in the free states . . . to let the slavery of the other states alone," but "we should never knowingly lend ourselves directly or indirectly, to prevent slavery from dying a natural death" (1:348). In other words, slavery, in Lincoln's mind, was a tolerable evil that, if ignored, would someday go away.

Indeed, Lincoln's earlier statements about slavery reveal that he was morally opposed to it but that he would not take any overt action against it. He was born into an antislavery family, living in the slave state of Kentucky, who migrated to free Indiana when Lincoln was a child. Ironically, two Lincoln biographers, Michael Burlingame and Allen C. Guelzo, suggest that Lincoln developed an early distaste for slavery because his father worked him like a slave on the family farm.[6] If that is true, Lincoln bears comparison to Mark Twain's most famous fictional character, Huckleberry Finn, who experiences bondage and excessively harsh treatment under his abusive father, Pap Finn. That experience prompts Huck to sympathize with Jim, the runaway slave, when the two meet at Jackson's Island and then head downriver on the raft for their famous journey and their stirring adventures.

As Lincoln grew into manhood, he became the embodiment of the self-made American. He left the toil of the family farm for better prospects in New Salem, Illinois. After trying several occupations, including boatman, surveyor, store clerk, and postmaster, Lincoln settled on the law and politics as a career. By the time he was twenty-eight years old, he had earned a license to practice law, and he had begun his political career as an Illinois legislator. These professional experiences might also have shaped Lincoln's attitude on slavery. He believed in the right to rise, the right to improve one's station in life as he had done. In a fragment of a speech probably composed during the late 1850s, Lincoln wrote, "We proposed to give *all* a chance; and we expected the weak to grow stronger, the ignorant wiser; and all better, and happier together" (2:222). Slavery, of course, contradicted that possibility. Most slaves remained in bondage for life; they could not do with their lives what Lincoln had done so impressively with his own. Slavery negated the American notion of opportunity for all and the American dream of achieving personal success and prosperity regardless of the circumstances of birth. An American slave could not become a Benjamin Franklin or an Abraham Lincoln.

Lincoln's first official action against slavery took place early in his political career, on March 3, 1837, when he joined with another Illinois legislator, Dan Stone, to issue a protest against slavery several weeks after the Illinois legislature passed a series of proslavery resolutions. Lincoln and Stone's protest stated that "the institution of slavery is founded on both injustice and bad policy." But their document also asserted that "the promulgation of abolition doctrines tends rather to increase than to abate its [slavery's] evils" (1:75). Their statement of protest also conceded that the Congress of the United States had no right to interfere with slavery where it already existed, except in the District of Columbia.

Lincoln's condemnation of the abolitionists was, if nothing else, politically prudent in Illinois in 1837. Douglas L. Wilson states that Lincoln and Stone's announcement that they were against abolitionists "was a pressing political necessity."[7] Nine years later, when Lincoln ran for Congress, he received 6,340 votes to his Democratic opponent's 4,829 votes. An abolitionist candidate on that ballot received only 249 votes.[8] The young politician Lincoln was shrewd enough to realize that the voters of Illinois would not support an abolitionist candidate, so, early in his career, he came out on record as opposing abolitionists.

But Lincoln opposed the abolitionists not only for political reasons; he was, by temperament, a conservative man who opposed social agitation that threatened the existing political and social order, a point he made very clearly in his speech before the Young Men's Lyceum in Springfield, Illinois, on January 27, 1838, the most important speech of his political career to that point. Lincoln opened that address by stating that the United States was currently experiencing a period of great satisfaction; the nation was blessed with fertile soil and fair climate and had established the best form of government on earth. This period of prosperity, however, was threatened, according to Lincoln, by domestic political discord—"the increasing disregard for law which pervades this country; the growing disposition to substitute the wild and furious passions, in lieu of the sober judgement of Courts; and the worse than savage mobs, for the executive ministers of justice" (1:109). As examples, Lincoln offered racially motivated violence in St. Louis and Vicksburg, Mississippi. Lincoln then put forth a stern rebuke of mob rule and recommended strict adherence to the laws of the land: "Let reverence for the laws, be breathed by every American mother, to the lisping babe, that prattles on her lap—let it be taught in schools, in seminaries, and in colleges;—let it be written in Primmers, spelling books, and Almanacs;—let it be preached from the pulpit, proclaimed in legislative halls, and enforced in courts of justice" (1:112).

Lincoln did not specifically mention the abolitionists in the Lyceum speech, but he clearly stated his opposition to the kind of civil unrest that some of the more radical abolitionists were advocating. He also opposed the kind of civil disobedience that Henry David Thoreau—and later Martin Luther King Jr.—would promote to deal with legally sanctioned injustice:

> When I so pressingly urge a strict observance of all the laws, let me not be understood as saying there are no bad laws, nor that grievances may not arise, for the redress of which, no legal provisions have been made. I mean to say no such thing. But I do mean to say, that, although bad laws, if they exist, should be repealed as soon as possible, still while they continue in force, for the sake of example, they should be religiously observed. (1:112)

For Lincoln in the late 1830s, an antiabolitionist posture was politically useful, but it was also one that he could defend on both moral and legal grounds.

Yet Lincoln remained strongly opposed to slavery, a position that he made clear in private and public statements. An often-quoted letter to Mary Speed in 1841 records Lincoln's distaste for all aspects of the institution of slavery. He wrote to Speed of his experience aboard a riverboat, when he saw twelve slaves being shipped downriver for sale at auction:

> They were chained six and six together. A small iron clevis was around the left wrist of each, and this fastened to the main chain by a shorter one at a convenient distance from, the others; so that the negroes were strung together precisely like so many fish upon a trot-line. In this condition they were being separated forever from the scenes of their childhood, their friends, their fathers and mothers, and brothers and sisters,

and many of them, from their wives and children, and going into perpetual slavery where the lash of the master is proverbially more ruthless and unrelenting than any other where. (1:260)

Here, in a few sentences, Lincoln identified slavery's many evils—the harsh treatment, the deprivation of freedom and accompanying lack of geographic mobility, the separation of families against their will. In contrast, Lincoln moves about the nation freely; the letter speaks of arrivals and departures made during his riverboat journey. In a public statement made several months after he wrote the letter to Speed—a speech delivered to the Springfield Washington Temperance Society— Lincoln likened the bondage of the alcoholic to the bondage of slavery and looked forward to the elimination of both—"when there shall be neither a slave nor a drunkard on the earth" (1:279).

At this time in his life, however, Lincoln was willing to do little more than make occasional statements about the evils of slavery. In fact, he was willing to profit personally from the institution. In 1847, Lincoln accepted the case of Robert Matson, a Kentucky slave owner who had brought one of his slaves, Jane Bryant, and her children to Illinois to work on a farm owned by Matson and run by Jane's husband, Anthony Bryant, a free man. After working in Illinois for two years, Jane had an argument with Matson's common-law wife, who threatened to sell Jane and her children downriver. Jane then declared herself a free woman because she had been living in a state where slavery was illegal. The case went to court. Lincoln represented Matson but lost the case, the judge ruling that Jane Bryant had lived long enough in a free state to be declared a free woman. Two years later, Lincoln represented his wife, Mary Todd Lincoln, and her sisters in their claims upon their deceased father's estate, which included the Todd family slaves.

David Herbert Donald suggests that Lincoln's involvement in cases like that of Matson should not be taken "as an indication of Lincoln's views on slavery; his business was law, not morality."[9] Benjamin Quarles excuses Lincoln for defending Matson's claim: "It is not easy to say why Lincoln consented to represent Robert Matson. Possibly he may have felt that even the devil was entitled to an advocate, that every litigant, no matter how unlovable, should have his day in court. . . . Lincoln could hardly be judged by one fall from grace."[10] But Lincoln's willingness to make profits from the institution of slavery—an institution that he had already criticized as an injustice—does suggest a disinclination to act upon his articulated moral positions. He was, still, in the late 1840s, a man who respected the legal status quo. Matson was a citizen and the law might be on his side, so he deserved legal representation. The Todd sisters had a legal right to their father's property and the law defined his slaves as property, so they had a right to reap the financial benefits of slavery.

Contrast Lincoln's decision to handle these two cases with the choices that John Woolman made a century earlier when he confronted slavery during the course of his professional duties. Early in his adult life, Woolman, an antislavery Quaker living in New Jersey, worked for an attorney as a scrivener, and he once was assigned the task of copying a purchase agreement for the sale of a slave. Woolman performed the duty but afterward felt guilty about taking part in the sale of a human. Several years later, Woolman was solicited by a man to compose the will of the man's dying brother, who owned slaves. When Woolman learned that the dying man wished to leave his slaves to his children, Woolman refused to write the will. "I told the Man, that I believed the Practice of continuing Slavery . . . was not right; and had a Scruple in my Mind against doing any Writings of that Kind," Woolman stated in his journal.[11] Lincoln, apparently, felt no such scruples about dealing with slaves while he performed his lawyerly duties; he confessed no misgivings in his writings about dealing with the Matson and Todd family slaves.

But Lincoln began speaking out more vocally about slavery during the 1848 election campaign. (He was not publicly silent about slavery until 1854, as Hofstadter suggests.)[12] In the 1848 campaign, Lincoln supported Zachary Taylor, the candidate backed by the Whigs. One reason for Lincoln's support for Taylor was Lincoln's belief that Taylor would prevent slavery from spreading to the United States territories, whereas Taylor's opponent, Lewis Cass, Lincoln believed, would not take steps to prevent the extension of slavery. In a speech in Lacon, Illinois, just before election day, Lincoln claimed that "the peace and prosperity of the country, and the limitation of slavery depended upon the election of a Whig Congress and Gen. Taylor" (2:14).

Before campaigning for Taylor, Lincoln had held a seat in Congress, where he had spent two years without drawing too much attention to himself. Guelzo points out that during Lincoln's tenure in the House of Representatives, a total of thirty-six speeches on slavery were delivered, but none by Lincoln.[13] Shortly before leaving Congress, Lincoln, in January 1849, did propose legislation to outlaw slavery in Washington, D.C., but he withdrew the proposed bill due to a lack of backers. Although Lincoln found the existence of slavery in the nation's capital to be a public embarrassment, he was not eager to back a losing proposition, even though he was about to leave office. Here again, Lincoln was unwilling to act upon a moral position.

At this point in his life, Lincoln's political idol was Henry Clay of Kentucky, a solid supporter of Whig policies. On the slavery question, Clay was a middle-of-the-roader. He owned slaves but sensed the danger that the institution would eventually bring upon the nation. In his eulogy on Clay, who died in 1852, Lincoln praised Clay's practical position on slavery:

> He ever was, on principle and in feeling, opposed to slavery. The very earliest, and one of the latest public efforts of his life, separated by a period of more than fifty years, were both made in favor of gradual emancipation of the slaves of Kentucky. He did not perceive, that on a question of human right, the negroes were to be excepted from the human race. And yet Mr. Clay was the owner of slaves. Cast into life where slavery was already widely spread and deeply seated, he did not perceive . . . how it could be at *once* eradicated, without producing a greater evil, even to the cause of human liberty itself. His feeling and his judgment, therefore, ever led him to oppose both extremes of opinion on the subject. (2:130)

By the time of Clay's death, Lincoln was back in Illinois, working hard as a lawyer and temporarily retired from politics. He returned to the political arena after the passage of the Kansas-Nebraska Act, the bill, pushed through Congress by Lincoln's fellow Illinoisan, Stephen Douglas, that potentially opened the Kansas-Nebraska territory to slavery. Douglas promoted the concept of popular sovereignty—allowing the local population of a territory to decide upon the question of slavery. Predictably, Douglas's legislation created a furor among Americans opposed to slavery.[14] The bill negated the Missouri Compromise of 1820, which had prohibited slavery in all United States territories north of the 36°30' latitude mark.

It is not hard to understand why the passage of the Kansas-Nebraska Act upset Lincoln. The bill seriously threatened his conservative and complacent position on slavery—that the institution would remain legal where it already existed, that it would not spread to new territories, and that it would eventually become extinct. If slavery could be introduced to new territory owned or acquired by the United States, it could, theoretically, become nationalized. The new territories would eventually become new states. The slave states would soon outnumber the free states in Congress and in the Electoral College. When the representatives from slave states took control of Congress, the presidency, and eventually the Supreme Court, proslavery legislation—even Constitutional amendments eternally perpetuating slavery and legalizing it in the North—would inevitably follow.

Quarles sees the passage of the Kansas-Nebraska Act in 1854 as Lincoln's "great awakening."[15] Waldo Braden analyzed the 175 speeches that Lincoln gave between 1854 and 1860 and concludes that Lincoln became a "one-issue man" on the slavery question during that time period.[16] During the late summer and early fall of 1854, Lincoln began to attack Douglas's legislation in a series of speeches in Illinois cities and towns. At Winchester, Carrollton, Bloomington, and Springfield, Lincoln sharply attacked the Kansas-Nebraska Act and called for a reinstatement of the repealed Missouri Compromise. At Bloomington, Lincoln called slavery "a moral, social and political evil" (2:239)—bold language that he had never before used in his criticism of slavery.

The most revealing speech of that time period is the one that Lincoln delivered in Peoria, Illinois, on October 16, 1854, which Neely sees as Lincoln's first great speech.[17] In this long address, Lincoln sounded themes that would propel him to national prominence during the next six years. He conceded that slavery should not be disturbed in the places where it already existed; early in the speech Lincoln stated, "I wish to MAKE and to KEEP the distinction between the EXISTING institution, and its EXTENSION of it, so broad, and so clear, that no honest man can misunderstand me, and no dishonest one, successfully misrepresent me" (2:248). But Lincoln was adamant in his opposition to extending slavery into new territories, a possibility resulting from the passage of the Kansas-Nebraska Act. Lincoln delivered a lengthy history of the issue of slavery and the United States territories; he claimed that the policy of prohibiting slavery in the territories began with Thomas Jefferson: "Thus, with the author of the Declaration of Independence, the policy of prohibiting slavery in new territory originated" (2:249). According to Lincoln, Jefferson's policy continued into the nineteenth century and received the blessing of Congress in 1820 with the passage of the Missouri Compromise: "The Missouri Compromise had been in practical operation for about a quarter of a century, and had received the sanction and approbation of men of all parties in every section of the Union" (2:251).

Lincoln went on to condemn the extension of slavery as both immoral and a violation of the democratic principles upon which the American republic was established:

> This *declared* indifference, but as I must think, covert *real* zeal for the spread of slavery, I can not but hate. I hate it because of the monstrous injustice of slavery itself. I hate it because it deprives our republican example of its just influence in the world—enables the enemies of free institutions, with plausibility, to taunt us as hypocrites—causes the real friends of freedom to doubt our sincerity, and especially because it forces so many really good men amongst ourselves into an open war with the very fundamental principles of civil liberty—criticizing the Declaration of Independence, and insisting that there is no right principle of action but *self-interest*. (2:255)

Not only is slavery immoral—a "monstrous injustice"—but it also violates the principles on which the United States stands. "Our republican robe is soiled, and trailed in the dust," he said later in the speech (2:276). Here, Lincoln identified a contradiction between the most sacred words of Jefferson's Declaration of Independence and the American republic as it now stands: "Nearly eighty years ago we began by declaring that all men are created equal; but now . . . we have run down to the other declaration, that for SOME men to enslave OTHERS is a 'sacred right of self-government.' These principles can not stand together" (2:275). Lincoln further asserted: "If the negro is a *man*, why then my ancient faith teaches me that 'all men are created equal;' and that there can be no moral right in connection with one man's making a slave of another" (2:266). According to Lincoln, "When the white man governs himself that is self-government; but when he governs himself, and also governs *another* man, that is *more* than self-government—that is despotism" (2:266).

Also evident in the Peoria speech, however, are contradictions that would prove difficult for Lincoln to resolve, a challenge that he would finally confront during his White House years. Although Lincoln embraced the abstract principle articulated in the Declaration of Independence that "all men are created equal," he was, at this moment, unable to accept the black American as a social and political equal and as a fellow citizen. He conceded that he did not know what to do with slavery where it already exists; his first impulse "would be to free all the slaves, and send them to Liberia,—to their own native land" (2:255). The overwhelming majority of slaves were, of course, Americans, not Africans. Lincoln, however, could not accept the slaves as his fellow citizens; he wished to send them "back" to their "native land." He also considered and rejected the abolitionist position: "Free them, and make them politically and socially our equals? My own feelings will not admit of this. . . . We can not, then, make them equals" (2:256). Lincoln based his opposition to slavery on the argument that all "men are created equal," but he simultaneously rejected the slave as an American citizen with equal social and political rights. *These* principles cannot stand together.

The Peoria speech also reveals Lincoln's political priorities at this stage of his political career. He pronounced slavery a great evil—"the great mass of mankind . . . consider slavery a great moral wrong" (2:281)—but worse evils existed in Lincoln's hierarchy of ills. At one point in the speech, Lincoln called the Constitution's three-fifths compromise "manifestly unfair." (For the purpose of determining the size of a state's congressional delegation, five slaves were counted as three residents.) But Lincoln will not "complain of it, in so far as it is already settled. It is in the constitution; and I do not, for that cause, or any other cause, propose to destroy, or alter, or disregard the constitution. I stand to it, fairly, fully and firmly" (2:269). Slavery was, of course, supported by the Constitution; abolishing slavery would require altering this sacred document, which Lincoln could not bring himself to do at this time. At Peoria, Lincoln also articulated his respect for the Union: "Much as I hate slavery, I would consent to the extension of it rather than see the Union dissolved, just as I would consent to any GREAT evil, to avoid a GREATER one" (2:270). But slavery is precisely the evil that is threatening the Union, "the only one thing which ever endangers the Union" (2:270). Nonetheless, Lincoln will tolerate slavery—even its extension—if that will prevent the dissolution of the Union. He will have to rethink that position during the Civil War.

At this time, when Lincoln was condemning slavery on both moral and political grounds, he was also using a lawyer's logic to build his argument against it. In a fragment on slavery that Lincoln probably wrote at about this time, he considered the issue of slavery in a series of "if-then" propositions:[18]

> If A. can prove, however conclusively, that he may, of right, enslave B.—why may not B. snatch the same argument, and prove equally, that he may enslave A?—
>
> You say A. is white, and B. is black. It is *color*, then; the lighter having the right to enslave the darker? Take care. By this rule, you are to be slave to the first man you meet, with a fairer skin than your own.
>
> You do not mean *color* exactly?—You mean the whites are *intellectually* the superiors of the blacks, and, therefore have the right to enslave them? Take care again. By this rule, you are to be slave to the first man you meet, with an intellect superior to your own. (2:222–23)

Thus, in Lincoln's mind slavery was wrong on moral grounds—an injustice that violated the sacred principles put forth in the Declaration of Independence; on political grounds—a threat to the peace and prosperity of the Union; and on logical grounds as well.

Certainly Lincoln's argument that the slavery issue would rend the

Union seemed valid. Violence erupted in Kansas between proslavery and antislavery settlers not long after the passage of the Kansas-Nebraska Act. For eighteen months, a civil war raged in Kansas, a conflict that would result in the loss of more than two hundred lives. In the autumn of 1856, a new governor, supported by three thousand federal troops, established order in Kansas, but the nation had become a powder keg ready to explode over the issue of slavery.

The next controversy concerning slavery was provided by the United States Supreme Court. In March 1857, the Court delivered its decision in the case of *Dred Scott v. Sandford*. Scott was a Missouri slave taken for a time by his master, John Emerson, to the free state of Illinois and the free territory of Minnesota. After Emerson died, Scott, claiming that he had become a free man while residing in free territory, sued Mrs. Emerson for his freedom. Scott appealed his case all the way to the Supreme Court but lost. In deciding the case, the Court, in a complicated opinion, considered and resolved three questions: Could Congress prohibit slavery in United States territories? Was Scott a United States citizen who could bring his case to the Court? Did Scott's residence in a free state and territory make him a free man?

On the question of Scott's citizenship, Chief Justice Roger Taney, writing for the Court, argued that the framers of the Constitution had not intended slaves and their descendants to be United States citizens, so Scott had no standing in any federal court. That ruling surely disheartened abolitionists, most of whom believed that all individuals born on United States soil were citizens. But the Court's resolution of the other two questions were, for abolitionists, even more problematic. The Court ruled that Congress could not outlaw slavery in any United States territory, a judgment that invalidated the Missouri Compromise of 1820. But probably the most disturbing component of the Court's ruling, for abolitionists, concerned the question of whether slaves would become free when their owners brought them into a free state or territory. In resolving that question, the Court ruled that a slave was a piece of property and that a United States citizen could not be denied property without due process; hence, Emerson retained ownership of Scott when he brought Scott to Minnesota and Illinois. "[N]either Dred Scott himself, nor any of his family, were made free by being carried into this territory [Minnesota]; even if they had been carried there by their owner, with the intention of becoming a permanent resident," wrote Taney.[19]

Why antislavery Americans would be greatly disturbed by the *Dred Scott* case is not hard to understand. First, Taney's decision opened all United States territories to slavery; it even nullified Stephen Douglas's notion of popular sovereignty because no act of Congress or federal initiative could limit slavery in the territories. Second, by identifying a slave as a piece of property protected by the Fifth Amendment to the Constitution, Taney's decision equated a slave with livestock or a horse or a wagon. If Missouri farmers could bring their cows to Illinois and retain possession of them, why could they not bring their slaves to Illinois and retain ownership of them? Given the decision in *Dred Scott*, how could the free states continue to prohibit slavery? And Taney also had ruled that it did not matter whether Scott were brought to a free territory for a day or permanently; Scott would remain a slave. A state or territorial constitution prohibiting slavery would be moot in that case.

Lincoln's sensed the danger and began to address it. In a speech in Springfield, Illinois, on June 26, 1857, Lincoln, at great length, criticized Taney's decision in *Dred Scott*, specifically Taney's assertion that the "created equal" clause of the Declaration of Independence and the guarantees of the Constitution do not apply to black Americans: "I had thought the Declaration promised something better than the condition of British subjects; but no, it only meant that we should be *equal* to them in their own oppressed and *unequal* condition. According to that, it gave no promise that having kicked off the King and Lords of Great Britain, we should not at once be saddled with a King and Lords of our own" (2:407). In Lincoln's view, the Declaration's "created equal" clause was a "maxim for a free society, which would be familiar to all, and revered by all; constantly looked to, constantly labored for, and even though never perfectly attained, constantly approximated, and thereby constantly spreading and deepening its influence, and augmenting the happiness and value of life to all people of all colors everywhere" (2:406). According to Guelzo, the Declaration of Independence provided for Lincoln "a moral theory from which to denounce slavery extension"; it became "a substitute scripture." Slavery was "a step away from the sacred document of the Founding, a step away from liberty and toward the enslavement of everyone."[20]

Lincoln articulated his fear of the ramifications of *Dred Scott* in a draft of a speech written sometime during the spring of 1858. For Lincoln, the "logical conclusion" of Taney's decision is the elimination of all restrictions against slavery anywhere in the United States: "what Dred Scott's master might lawfully do with Dred in the free State of Illinois, every other master may lawfully do with any other one or one hundred slaves in Illinois, or in any other free State" (2:453). A short time later, in his famous House Divided speech, Lincoln would express his fear that a follow-up Supreme Court decision would declare "that the Constitution of the United States does not permit a *state* to exclude slavery from its limits" (2:467).

David Zarefsky suggests that Lincoln was hardly farfetched in his thinking on this point. By the time of the *Dred Scott* decision, the case of *Lemmon v. the People* was already working its way through the New York courts. The case involved a Virginia slave owner who had brought eight slaves to New York to be shipped, from there, to Texas. The New York state supreme court had ruled that the slaves were immediately free when they reached free soil, but the owner had appealed the decision. If the case reached Taney's Supreme Court, he would likely rule as he did in *Dred Scott*—that the eight slaves remained their owner's property when they arrived in New York. Such a decision would certainly open the free states to slavery. According to Zarefsky, the *Lemmon* case was nationally known, and it is quite possible that Lincoln was aware of it, at least by the time of his debates with Stephen Douglas in 1858.[21]

Lincoln's 1858 House Divided speech, delivered to kick off his Senate campaign against Douglas, was arguably the most noteworthy speech delivered before his presidency. It was certainly one of the most forceful in terms of his criticism of slavery. Don E. Fehrenbacher calls it "one of those moments of synthesis which embody the past and illumine the future."[22] Lincoln opened his speech by referring to the four-year-old policy, initiated by the Kansas-Nebraska Act, of opening the United States territories to slavery. This policy, instead of settling the slavery question, had the reverse outcome—"agitation has not only, *not ceased*, but has *constantly augmented*." That agitation, according to Lincoln, "*will* not cease, until a *crisis* shall have been reached, and passed" (2:461). Then he framed his argument with a biblical reference:

> "A house divided against itself cannot stand."
> I believe this government cannot endure, permanently half *slave* and half *free*.
> I do not expect the Union to be *dissolved*—I do not expect the house to *fall*—but I *do* expect it will cease to be divided.
> It will become *all* one thing, or *all* the other.
> Either the *opponents* of slavery, will arrest the further spread of it, and place it where the public mind shall rest in the belief that it is in course of ultimate extinction; or its *advocates* will push it forward, till it shall become alike lawful in *all* the States, *old* as well as *new*—*North* as well as *South*. (2:461–62)

The rest of the House Divided speech examined themes that Lincoln had articulated during the previous four years—his opposition to the Kansas-Nebraska Act, his criticism of Douglas's notion of popular sovereignty, his denouncement of the *Dred Scot* decision. He presented the scenario of the American house becoming all slave: "We shall *lie down* pleasantly dreaming that the people of *Missouri* are on the verge of making their State *free*; and we shall *awake* to the *reality*, instead, that the *Supreme* Court has made *Illinois* a *slave* State" (2:467). Lincoln speculated that the African slave trade, the importation of slaves to the United States, which was outlawed after 1807 by an act of Congress, would resume because slave owners will be deemed to have "a sacred right" to purchase slaves "where they can be bought cheapest" (2:468). Lincoln then pledged, with the help of like-minded citizens, to avoid this drift toward national slavery: "We shall not fail—if we stand firm, we shall not fail" (2:468).

Lincoln had never before phrased the slavery debate into such apocalyptic language. He seemed to be predicting a struggle between North and South over slavery that would lead to complete victory for one side and a devastating defeat for the other. No longer was he advocating a policy of containment—permitting slavery to exist where it was already entrenched, preventing slavery's expansion into new territories, and allowing the institution to die a natural death at some indefinite time in the future. He seemed to be moving away from the middle of the road and embracing the abolitionist cause—making the United States a house free from slavery.

During the 1858 Senate campaign, however, Lincoln backed off the hard-line position articulated in the House Divided speech. Perhaps he sensed that he had gone too far in opposing slavery for his own political good. Perhaps he was troubled by the obvious conclusion of his house divided argument—that a Union-rending conflict over slavery was inevitable. For Lincoln, at this time, slavery was surely an evil, but the dissolution of the Union, the collapse of the divided house, was worse; he was not relishing, in 1858, the prospect of a civil war over slavery. Hofstadter suggests that possibly Lincoln's mind was a house divided against itself or possibly that he was merely "a professional politician looking for votes."[23] At any rate, he moved back toward the center of the road.

After hearing of the House Divided speech, Douglas accused Lincoln of promoting a war between North and South over slavery. In a campaign speech in Chicago on July 10, a few weeks after the House Divided speech, Lincoln responded to Douglas by trying to calm his audience's concern over his forceful language of that earlier speech. He rejected Douglas's claim that he was advocating war: "I only said what I expected would take place. I made a prediction only—it may have been a foolish one perhaps" (2:491). He repeated his noninterference policy, which he seemed to reject in the House Divided speech: "I have said a hundred times, and I have no inclination to take it back, that I believe there is no right, and ought to be no inclination in the people of the free States to enter the slave States, and interfere with the question of slavery at all. I have said that always" (2:492). Lincoln also sounded his familiar arguments against the extension of slavery into the territories and for the inclusion of African Americans under the "created equal" clause of the Declaration of Independence, but he obviously had backed away from the forceful language of the House Divided speech.

Later in the campaign, Lincoln restated his middle-of-the-road position on slavery. In a speech at Springfield, Lincoln repeated his policy of noninterference: "I have again and again said that I would not enter into any of the States to disturb the institution of slavery" (2:513). Referring to his prediction that the United States would eventually become either all free or all slave, he stated, "I did not express my *wish* on anything. In that passage I indicated no wish or purpose of my own; I simply expressed my *expectation*. Cannot the Judge [Douglas] perceive the distinction between a *purpose* and an *expectation*. I have often expressed an expectation to die, but I have never expressed a *wish* to die" (2:514). Clearly Lincoln wanted to sound a moderate tone during his campaign with Douglas because, as Zarefsky suggests, "[o]nly a moderate would have a chance of building a winning coalition."[24]

Zarefsky notes that the political culture of Illinois was, in 1858, "a microcosm of the nation."[25] Its northern counties were antislavery, while its southern counties, which bordered the slave states of Missouri and Kentucky, contained many proslavery settlers. The geographic middle of the state was politically moderate. A successful politician in Illinois in 1858 would have to appeal to those moderate voters in central Illinois. Hence, Douglas and Lincoln each attempted to push his opponent toward the political extreme. Douglas accused Lincoln of being an abolitionist and of inciting a civil war between North and South over the slavery question. Lincoln countered by accusing Douglas of being part of a conspiracy to nationalize slavery under the benign notion of popular sovereignty. The conspiracy involved Presidents Franklin Pierce and James Buchanan, both of whom supported Douglas's popular sovereignty, Chief Justice Taney, and Douglas. More than once during the campaign, Lincoln depicted these four as carpenters fitting together the timbers and mortises of a house—the house of slavery that Lincoln had introduced in the House Divided speech.

In the famous debates between Lincoln and Douglas during the 1858 campaign, both candidates attempted to appeal to the centrist voters. During the first three debates, Lincoln sounded themes now familiar to the Illinois electorate—his fear of the nationalization of slavery resulting from a follow-up decision to *Dred Scott*, his pledge not to interfere with slavery where it already existed, and his concern that the nation's current crisis over slavery was the inevitable result of opening the territories to slaveholders. To appeal to the proslavery voter, Lincoln even gave his support to the Fugitive Slave Law, a bill that abolitionists found particularly distasteful. "I do not now, nor ever did, stand in favor of the unconditional repeal of the fugitive slave law," Lincoln said in his second debate with Douglas (3:40). In that debate, he also claimed that he was not pledged to the abolition of slavery in the District of Columbia or to the prohibition of the slave trade between states. Astonishingly, Lincoln stated that he was not pledged against the admission of new slave states into the Union (3:40). In the fourth debate, Lincoln reached back to express his earlier belief that slavery would ultimately disappear from the United States "in God's own good time" (3:181).

In the fifth debate, however, Lincoln introduced the moral argument against slavery. He attacked Douglas for saying that he did not care whether slavery was voted up or down in a territory or state. He accused Douglas of seeing nothing wrong with slavery, a moral insensitivity that might jar moderate Illinois voters. Lincoln tried to draw a contrast between himself and Douglas on moral grounds:

> Now, I confess myself as belonging to that class in the country who contemplate slavery as a moral, social and political evil, having due regard for its actual existence amongst us and the difficulties of getting rid of it in any satisfactory way, and to all the constitutional obligations which have been thrown about it; but, nevertheless, desire a policy that looks to the prevention of it as a wrong, and looks hopefully to the time when as a wrong it may come to an end. (3:226)

Zarefsky is correct when he states that Lincoln and Douglas rarely brought the question of the morality of slavery into their debates, but Lincoln is arguably most effective when he attacks Douglas's moral insensitivity to the plight of slaves.[26]

In the final two debates, Douglas hit back hard by returning to Lincoln's House Divided speech. He tried to point out the apparent contradiction between Lincoln's previously stated position of noninterference with slavery where it existed and his assertion in the House Divided speech that the nation must eventually become all slave or all free:

> Down in the southern part of the State he [Lincoln] takes the ground openly that he will not interfere with slavery where it exists, and says that he is not now and never was in favor of interfering with slavery where it exists in the States. Well, if he is not in favor of that, how does he expect to bring slavery in a course of ultimate extinction? . . . How can he extinguish it in Kentucky, in Virginia, in all the slave States by his policy, if he will not pursue a policy which will interfere with it in the States where it exists? (3:265)

Sensing a winning argument, Douglas repeated it with stronger language in the seventh and final debate. He again asked how Lincoln would put slavery on a course toward ultimate extinction if he pledged not to interfere with the institution where it already exists. Douglas answered his own question by portraying Lincoln as the destroyer of the South:

> His idea is that he will prohibit slavery in all the territories, and thus force them all to become free States, surrounding the slave States with a cordon of free States, and hemming them in, keeping the slaves confined to their present limits whilst they go on multiplying until the soil on which they live will no longer feed them, and he will thus be able to put slavery in a course of ultimate extinction by starvation. . . . He will extinguish slavery in the Southern States as the French general exterminated the Algerines when he smoked them out. He is going to extinguish slavery by surrounding the slave States, hemming in the slaves, and starving them out of existence as you smoke a fox out of his hole. (3:323)

Douglas had hit upon obvious contradictions in Lincoln's thinking about slavery. If slavery were indeed evil, a blight on America's charter of freedom, then how could it be tolerated even for one minute longer where it exists? Should not a man who viewed slavery as evil be an abolitionist? Would not a man who believed slavery to be a moral wrong and who also believed that his nation cannot continue half slave and half free work to make his nation completely free? Was a middle-of-the-road position on slavery possible in 1858?

Lincoln would continue to grapple with these contradictions for the next three years. He would remain steadfast in his condemnation of slavery as a great moral wrong. He would maintain his pledge of non-interference with slavery in the slave states but oppose the extension of slavery into the territories. He would continue to support the Fugitive Slave Law because the retrieval of refugee slaves was guaranteed by Article IV of the Constitution. He would hope for slavery's ultimate extinction but remain aware that taking overt action toward that end would destroy the Union or lead the nation to civil war. This divided man would remain in the divided house and hope that it would not fall.

After his defeat by Douglas, Lincoln wrote to a client to comment on the campaign. "I am glad I made the late race," Lincoln stated. "It gave me a hearing on the great and durable question of the age, which I could have had in no other way; and though I now sink out of view, and shall be forgotten, I believe I have made some marks which will tell for the cause of liberty long after I am gone" (3:339). Lincoln, of course, would not sink out of view. Early in 1859, he was again on the speech circuit, reiterating the themes of the recent Senate campaign. By this time, Lincoln was indeed a one-issue politician. The Whig Party had broken up, and its agenda—protective tariffs, internal improvements, a national bank—had been filed away. Slavery was the issue foremost on the minds of virtually all Americans, and Lincoln was anxious to address it. He spoke in Chicago in March; in Council Bluffs, Iowa, in August; in Columbus and Dayton, Ohio, in September; in Indianapolis later that month; in Beloit and Janesville, Wisconsin, in October. Before the year's end, he made more speeches in Illinois, then traveled to Kansas. He arranged for the publication of the transcripts of the debates with Douglas. He wanted his ideas to circulate nationally. Of course, Lincoln had his eye on the White House.

In February 1860, Lincoln traveled to New York to deliver the speech that would propel him to the Republican nomination and toward the presidency. Originally scheduled for a church, Lincoln's lecture was moved to the Cooper Institute in Manhattan to accommodate the large crowd that was expected. The event provided Lincoln the opportunity to present his views to an audience from the North-east, folks who, perhaps, did not know well the Illinois politician who had challenged Douglas for his Senate seat. As a whole, the easterners would be harsher on slavery than Lincoln's fellow Illinoisans; Lincoln would not have to temper his criticism of the institution in any way before a New York audience.

When Lincoln spoke at Cooper Institute, the nation's mood was even more anxious than it had been during the election campaign of 1858. In October 1859, John Brown had led his unsuccessful raid on the federal arsenal in Harpers Ferry, Virginia. His goal had been to arm the nearby slaves and ignite a slave rebellion that would spread throughout the South and rid the nation of slavery forever. Brown was found guilty of murder and treason and executed in December. Fierce debate over the Brown affair broke out in the halls of Congress. Three days after Brown's death, Thaddeus Stevens, an abolitionist Pennsylvania congressman, was attacked with a knife by William Barksdale, a colleague from Mississippi, while the House was in session. In that instance, representatives quickly intervened to avert a tragedy but continued to come to work armed, ready for a civil war to break out in the legislative halls.

Lincoln began the Cooper Institute address with a long and elaborate argument to reach the conclusion that the framers of the Constitution did not intend it to prohibit federal control of slavery in the territories. Here Lincoln was on safe ground; appealing to the desires of the "Founding Fathers" in a time of national crisis is usually a winning argument. According to Lincoln, Americans should "supplant the opinions and policy of our fathers" only "upon evidence so conclusive, and argument so clear, that even their great authority, fairly considered and weighed, cannot stand" (3:535). Then Lincoln shifted his direction and his tone: "And now, if they would listen—as I suppose they will not—I would address a few words to the Southern people" (3:535).

Rather than offer his hand in friendship to the South at a time of national strife, Lincoln launched an assault. First, he categorically refuted recent charges made by the South against the Republican Party. The Republicans are not a sectional party. They are not revolutionaries; they wish to return to the status quo of the early 1850s, before the passage of the Kansas-Nebraska Act. According to Lincoln, John Brown's raid was not backed by Republicans; Southerners have used Brown to "break up the Republican organization" (3:541). The South, not the Republicans or radicals like Brown, poses the greatest threat to the Union: "Your purpose, then, plainly stated, is, that you will destroy the Government, unless you be allowed to construe and enforce the Constitution as you please, on all points in dispute between you and us. You will rule or ruin in all events" (3:543).

Lincoln also explored the issue of slavery's relationship to the Constitution. In some earlier speeches, he had implied that the Constitution protected slavery, and he had stated clearly his unwillingness to alter the Constitution in any way. But at Cooper Institute, Lincoln reiterated a point that he had made in the final debate with Douglas in 1858—that "the right of property in a slave is not *'distinctly* and *expressly* affirmed' in it [the Constitution]" (3:544); he went further, arguing that the authors of the Constitution wished to exclude the idea of slavery from the document:

> [I]t would be open to others to show that neither the word "slave" nor "slavery" is to be found in the Constitution, nor the word "property" even, in any connection with language alluding to the things slave, or slavery, and that wherever in that instrument the slave is alluded to, he is called a "person;"—and wherever his master's legal right in relation to him is alluded to, it is spoken of as "service or labor which may be due,"—as a debt payable in service or labor. Also, it would be open to show, by contemporaneous history, that this mode of alluding to slaves and slavery, instead of speaking of them, was employed on purpose to exclude from the Constitution the idea that there could be property in man. (3:545)

Here for the first time, Lincoln suggested that slavery might be incompatible with the principles and provisions of the Constitution.

Near the end of his speech, Lincoln seemed to indicate that he saw no possibility of easing the tensions between North and South. He asked what would satisfy the South, then provided a troubling response:

> This, and this only: cease to call slavery *wrong* and join them in calling it *right*. And this must be done thoroughly—done in *acts* as well as in

words. Silence will not be tolerated—we must place ourselves avowedly with them. Senator Douglas's new sedition law must be enacted and enforced, suppressing all declarations that slavery is wrong, whether made in politics, in presses, in pulpits, or in private. We must arrest and return their fugitive slaves with greedy pleasure. We must pull down our Free State constitutions. The whole atmosphere must be disinfected from all taint of opposition to slavery, before they will cease to believe that all their troubles proceed from us. (3:547–48)

In other words, Lincoln charged that the South demanded nothing less from the North than complete capitulation on the slavery issue. Unwilling to capitulate to the South's demands, Lincoln concluded with a call to arms to his fellow Republicans in their conflict with the South over slavery: "Neither let us be slandered from our duty by false accusations against us, nor frightened from it by menaces of destruction to the Government nor of dungeons to ourselves. LET US HAVE FAITH THAT RIGHT MAKES MIGHT, AND IN THAT FAITH, LET US, TO THE END, DARE TO DO OUR DUTY AS WE UNDERSTAND IT" (3:550).

Never before had Lincoln taken such a firm stance against the proponents of slavery. In Illinois, he had tempered his attacks on slavery, perhaps because he needed the votes of proslavery Illinoisans. Here in New York, in February 1860, with members of the eastern abolitionist wing of the Republican Party in attendance, Lincoln felt free to launch a forceful attack against the South and the supporters of slavery. He would need the support of antislavery men like those in this audience at the Republican convention in Chicago later in the year. This speech helped Lincoln garner their support; it made him a national force in the Republican Party and a serious candidate for the presidency in the election of 1860.

Lincoln gave several more speeches between the Cooper Institute speech and the Republican convention, held in May. In Providence, Rhode Island; in Manchester and Dover, New Hampshire; in Hartford and New Haven, Connecticut; and back home in Bloomington, Illinois, Lincoln drove home the now familiar Republican themes. For the Hartford speech, delivered on March 5, 1860, Lincoln developed

two analogies that, in his mind, helped to resolve an obvious contradiction in his antislavery rhetoric—his stated position that slavery
was a moral wrong but that it could continue where it was already
firmly in place. The first analogy concerned a snake:

> For instance, out in the street, or in the field, or on the prairie I find
> a rattlesnake. I take a stake and kill him. Everybody would applaud the
> act and say I did right. But suppose the snake was in a bed where children
> were sleeping. Would I do right to strike him there? I might hurt the
> children; or I might not kill, but only arouse and exasperate the snake,
> and he might bite the children. Thus, by meddling with him here, I
> would do more hurt than good. Slavery is like this. We dare not strike at
> it where it is. The manner in which our constitution is framed con-
> strains us from making war upon it where it already exists. The question
> that we now have to deal with is, "Shall we be acting right to take this
> snake and carry it to a bed where there are children?" The Republican
> party insists upon keeping it out of the bed. (4:5)

Lincoln equates slavery with the snake, the biblical symbol of evil.
The bed is the South, where slavery now exists. If that evil is disturbed
where it now lies, a greater evil might ensue, so it is best left alone.
But Lincoln's snake analogy has one obvious flaw. He assumes that
the snake does no immediate damage where it now lies; if it were
harming the children, surely their parents would be compelled to attack it forcefully. But can the same be said of slavery? Was it doing no
harm where it was currently in place? Lincoln maintained that slavery
was a moral wrong. How could he justify allowing it to remain where
it already existed if it were doing harm? The snake analogy did not
resolve Lincoln's contradiction.

The second analogy presented in the Hartford speech was more effective. Lincoln described seeing a man on a train with a large wen, or
boil, on his neck. "That wen represents slavery," said Lincoln; "it bears
the same relation to that man that slavery does to the country. That
wen is a great evil; the man that bears it will say so. But he does not
dare to cut it out. He bleeds to death if he does. If he does *not* cut it
out; it will shorten his life materially" (4:5–6). The mere existence of
the wen will shorten the man's life; yet immediately lancing it will

cause, perhaps, a problem of equal or even greater severity. The analogy of the wen would help Lincoln's audience understand and sympathize with his difficult position on the slavery issue. In Lincoln's view, the nation would be better off if slavery were removed from its soil, but removing it might result in a good deal of bloodshed.

At their national convention in Chicago in May, the Republicans nominated Lincoln for president. Zarefsky suggests that the Republicans had found a "safe" candidate—one who stood for checking slavery's advance but not for extending political and social rights to African Americans.[27] Once he accepted the nomination, Lincoln, adhering to political custom, did not campaign on his own behalf. In 1860, leading members of the parties, not the presidential candidates, ran the campaign and brought the party's platform to the voters, just as Lincoln had done for Zachary Taylor in the election of 1848. (Stephen Douglas, Lincoln's Democratic opponent, broke with tradition by campaigning on his own behalf in 1860.) Shortly after his nomination, Lincoln did write a short campaign autobiography for publication, but, strangely enough, this document does not discuss Lincoln's stand on slavery. It explains his opposition to the Mexican War and notes his support for Taylor in the presidential campaign of 1848. The autobiography refers to his temporary withdrawal from political life in the early 1850s and attributes Lincoln's return to politics to the repeal of the Missouri Compromise in 1854, which "aroused him as he had never been before" (4:67), but the document fails to present his views on slavery. Why a campaign autobiography, written to be read by voters during the election campaign of 1860, would not present a candidate's views on the nation's most pressing problem is a mystery. Perhaps Lincoln, respecting the tradition that the presidential candidates should remain aloof from the political fray, wished not to mention in his campaign autobiography the issue that was tearing apart the nation.

After his victory in the November election, Lincoln wanted to keep a low political profile. President James Buchanan and congressional leaders were attempting to deal with the secession crisis, which had developed immediately after Lincoln's election. In private statements, Lincoln tried to ease away from the hard-line positions that he had presented in the Cooper Institute speech. He wrote a passage for a speech to be delivered by Senator Lyman Trumbull of Illinois to assure the South that a Lincoln administration would cause the region no harm. Lincoln's passage stated that "the States will be left in as complete control of their own affairs respectively, and at as perfect liberty to choose, and employ, their own means of protecting property, and preserving peace and order within their respective limits, as they have ever been under any administration" (4:141). A few days before Christmas, Lincoln wrote to Representative Alexander Stephens of Georgia to reiterate his stated policy of noninterference with slavery in the South: "Do the people of the South really entertain fears that a Republican administration would, *directly* or *indirectly*, interfere with their slaves, or with them, about their slaves? If they do, I wish to assure you, as once a friend, and still, I hope, not an enemy, that there is no cause for such fears" (4:160).

But Lincoln also privately informed Republicans in Congress that during their discussions with Southern colleagues about the secession crisis, no compromise should be made regarding slavery in the territories. "Let there be no compromise on the question of *extending* slavery," he wrote Trumbull in December. On February 1, 1861, as the secession crisis worsened, Lincoln, in a letter to William H. Seward, stuck to that position: "I say now, however, as I have all the while said, that on the territorial question—that is, the question of extending slavery under the national auspices,—I am inflexible. I am for no compromise which *assists* or *permits* the extension of the institution on soil owned by the nation" (4:183).

Lincoln held firmly to that position as inauguration day approached. On his way to Washington, he broke a self-imposed silence on the secession crisis and made several short speeches at stops along the train route. For a speech to be delivered in Kentucky, Lincoln explained that he would refuse to compromise his position on the extension of slavery not only because it was his central campaign promise but because the principle of popular government demanded his refusal:[28]

> I so refused, not from any party wantonness, nor from any indifference to the troubles of the country. I thought such refusal was demanded by

the view that if, when a Chief Magistrate is constitutionally elected, he cannot be inaugurated till he betrays those who elected him, by breaking his pledges, and surrendering to those who tried and failed to defeat him at the polls, this government and all popular government is already at end. Demands for such surrender, once recognized, are without limit. . . . They break the only bond of faith between public and public servant; and they distinctly set the minority over the majority. (4:201)

Fehrenbacher states that Lincoln consistently "affirmed adherence to the most critical and most fragile principle in the democratic process—namely, the requirement of minority submission to majority will."[29] Almost twenty-five years earlier, in the Young Men's Lyceum speech, Lincoln had expressed his belief that activist minorities posed the most dangerous threat to democratic government; now, as Lincoln prepared for his inauguration, he was reiterating that point. He was fairly elected on a nonextension platform; he would attempt to implement that policy when he reached the White House.

Nonetheless, as he arrived in Washington, Lincoln was well aware of the danger to the Union posed by the secession crisis. Publicly, even before his inauguration, he felt the need to reassure the South that he did not intend to promote an abolitionist program. Responding to an official welcome by the mayor of Washington, D.C., which, in 1861, was a Southern city where slavery was legal, Lincoln tried to initiate a peace process between the two sections of his divided nation:

I have not now, and never have had, any disposition to treat you in any respect otherwise than as my own neighbors. I have not now any purpose to withhold from you any of the benefits of the constitution, under any circumstances, that I would not feel myself constrained to withhold from my own neighbors; and I hope, in a word, when we shall become better acquainted—and I say it with great confidence—we shall like each other the more. (4:246–47)

Lincoln was trying to abate the crisis that was enveloping the nation by asserting that the South's constitutional right to own human property would not be abridged during his administration. As inauguration day approached, Lincoln wanted the South to grasp that message.

Phillip Shaw Paludan calls Lincoln's First Inaugural Address "a plea for the status quo."[30] Lincoln opened the address by assuring the South that his administration would not interfere with slavery where it already existed; he repeated a statement from an earlier speech to make that point: "I have no purpose, directly or indirectly, to interfere with the institution of slavery in the States where it exists. I believe I have no lawful right to do so, and I have no inclination to do so" (4:263). He quoted a passage from Article IV of the Constitution to assure the South that the Fugitive Slave Law would remain in force: "No person held to service or labor in one State, under the laws thereof, escaping into another, shall, in consequence of any law or regulation therein, be discharged from such service or labor, but shall be delivered up on claim of the party to whom such service or labor may be due" (4:263). He also granted that the slavery issue involved difficult constitutional questions: "Shall fugitives from labor be surrendered by national or by State authority? The Constitution does not expressly say. *May* Congress prohibit slavery in the territories? The Constitution does not expressly say. *Must* Congress protect slavery in the territories? The Constitution does not expressly say" (4:267). By not advancing specific positions on these questions, Lincoln was opening the possibility for compromise between North and South.

Lincoln did express his disagreement with the South on the secession issue. "I hold, that in contemplation of universal law, and of the Constitution, the Union of these States is perpetual," he said. "Perpetuity is implied, if not expressed, in the fundamental law of all national governments" (4:264). And he conceded that the North and South differ on the crucial issue of slavery: "One section of our country believes slavery is *right,* and ought to be extended, while the other believes it is *wrong,* and ought not to be extended. This is the only substantial dispute" (4:269). But he pledged not to wage war to inflict his views on slavery upon the South: "The government will not assail *you.* You can have no conflict, without being yourselves the aggressors" (4:271). He concluded by extending an olive branch to the South by appealing, in lyrical prose, to the common patriotism and common history of the conflicting regions:

I am loth to close. We are not enemies, but friends. We must not be enemies. Though passion may have strained, it must not break our bonds of affection. The mystic chords of memory, stretching from every battle-field, and patriot grave, to every living heart and hearthstone, all over this broad land, will yet swell the chorus of the Union, when again touched, as surely they will be, by the better angels of our nature. (4:271)

"[W]here was the moral element, the injustice of slavery that had been so compelling in his prewar speeches?" asks Paludan of this address.[31] Lincoln presented no ringing condemnation of slavery or the South. Compared to the Cooper Institute speech, the First Inaugural was conciliatory in tone and content. Lincoln issued no call to arms here. He seemed to reject the prediction put forth in the House Divided speech that the American house must become ultimately all slave or all free. Perhaps Lincoln, as he began his presidency, had realized the truth of the old political adage that a candidate can campaign on either the left or right side of the political spectrum but, once elected, must govern from the center. Perhaps in reaching out to the South at this tumultuous moment Lincoln was revealing his own moral hierarchy at this point in his life and political career: Keeping the Union together was far more important than resolving the slavery question. Zarefsky points out that "the moral aspect of slavery was not the only value in his hierarchy. He gave special weight to the sanctity of the Constitution and the preservation of the Union"—both of which are stressed in the First Inaugural Address.[32] Reinhold Niebuhr makes a similar point: "In the political order justice takes an uneasy second place behind the first place of the value of internal order. In reviewing Lincoln's hierarchy of values, one must come to the conclusion that his sense of justice was strong enough to give that value an immediate position under the first purpose of national survival."[33]

Even so, the man from Illinois had come a long way on the slavery issue. He had begun his political career unconcerned with it. During the 1830s and 1840s, as the nation began debating slavery, Lincoln had remained focused on economic issues like the tariff, the national bank, and internal improvements. Slavery had not come to his corner of the world, so he had paid little attention to it. The passage of the Kansas-

Nebraska Act startled Lincoln from his complacency; a few years later, the *Dred Scott* decision threatened to bring slavery to his doorstep in Illinois. At that point, he began to address the issue, to articulate moral and political arguments in opposition to it.

Yet Lincoln did not join forces with the abolitionists. He mistrusted political reform movements, believing that the turmoil they created did the nation more harm than good. He expressed his hope that slavery would one day disappear, but he remained unwilling to take bold steps to uproot it. In 1861, he was of the same mind on slavery that he was in 1854, when he stated that he was "arguing against the EXTENSION of a bad thing, which where it already exists, we must of necessity, manage as best we can" (2:266). He found in the policy of nonextension of slavery a politically and morally comfortable position. He was taking a stand against a moral wrong, but his stand, he hoped, would neither offend the Constitution nor destroy the Union. At the start of his presidency, Lincoln, under incredible pressure to compromise, stuck to his position. He had won a fair election, and in line with the principles of popular government, he expected, as president, to turn position into policy.

Martin Duberman calls the nonextension position held by Lincoln and others "the perfect device for balancing . . . multiple needs"—the desire to put slavery on the course of ultimate extinction, the need to protect the property rights of Southerners and thereby ensure the stability of the Union, the necessity of keeping the existing slaves in bondage so that they would not flood the North and take jobs from working-class whites. The policy of nonextension, according to Duberman, "seemed a panacea, a formula which promised in time to do everything while for the present risked nothing. But like all panaceas, it ignored certain hard realities."[34]

Those hard realities would become apparent shortly after Lincoln's inauguration. By the time he took the oath of office on March 4, 1861, seven Southern states had already voted to withdraw from the Union; four more would eventually follow. Lincoln had hoped in his First Inaugural Address to offer the South a gesture of friendship and reconciliation. But just as Lincoln and his followers believed that the South was working to nationalize slavery, anti-Lincoln Southerners believed that he and his party were ready to implement a plan to uproot slavery from the entire continent. According to Southerners, execution of the nonextension policy would result in several more free states entering the Union. The North, in 1861, already dominated the House of Representatives; it would control the Senate when a few more free states joined the Union. With a large majority of electoral votes, the North would be able to keep antislavery men in the White House, who would appoint antislavery justices to the Supreme Court. Supreme Court decisions and perhaps new constitutional amendments to restrict slavery further inevitably would follow. In a generation, slavery might become illegal in the United States. Lincoln's words in his First Inaugural Address masked hard realities that the South was not ready or willing to accept in 1861. Its response was secession.

Lincoln, at this point in his life and political career, was still willing—even hoping—to compromise on slavery. Though he considered it a great evil, he would let it remain in half the country. In exchange, he hoped to buy peace, political stability, the status quo; most of all, perhaps, he hoped to preserve the American system of popular government. There is truth in Paludan's suggestion that Lincoln believed so strongly in the American system of government because he was a successful product of it.[35] That system of government had propelled him to the nation's highest office. He would realize during the next four years, however, that maintaining slavery and preserving the Union were incompatible goals. Four years later, on March 4, 1865, in his Second Inaugural Address, he would identify slavery as the very cause of the war of disunion. He was not yet able to see that—or at least articulate that idea in public—in March of 1861.

TWO

Lincoln's Racial Attitudes:
"We Can Not Make Them Our Equals"

IN 1848, Illinois voters considered new articles for a state constitution. One article submitted to the electorate would make it illegal for black Americans, slaves or freemen, to settle permanently in Illinois. More than 70 percent of the voters approved this measure, the vote going 50,261 for and 21,297 against.[1] That vote was hardly surprising in a state that Stephen B. Oates describes as "anti-Negro to the core" in Abraham Lincoln's time.[2] In Illinois during the 1840s, African Americans could not vote, run for public office, attend public schools, testify against white people or sue in court, own property, or serve in the state militia. Black Illinoisans were not considered state citizens. Stephen Douglas articulated the beliefs of many white residents of Illinois during his 1858 debates with Lincoln, when he stated:

> I hold that a negro is not and never ought to be a citizen of the United States. . . . I hold that this government was made on the white basis, by white men, for the benefit of white men and their posterity forever, and should be administered by white men and none others. I do not believe that the Almighty made the negro capable of self-government. . . . Now, I say to you, my fellow-citizens, that in my opinion the signers of the Declaration had no reference to the negro whatever when they declared all men to be created equal. They desired to express by that phrase, white men, men of European birth and European descent, and had no reference either to the negro, the savage Indians, the Fejee, the Malay, or

any other inferior and degraded race, when they spoke of the equality of
men. (3:112–13)

During the 1840s and 1850s, Douglas was the most popular politician in Illinois. He served in the Illinois state legislature from 1836
through 1838, held a seat on the state Supreme Court from 1841
through 1843, represented the state in the House of Representatives
from 1843 through 1847, and served as an Illinois senator in the
United States Senate from 1847 until his death in 1861. Douglas did
not enjoy a quarter century of political success by embracing attitudes
outside the political mainstream. His expressed views on racial issues
reflected those of a great majority of the residents of Illinois.

Illinois's initial constitution of 1818 prohibited slavery, but that
fact should not imply that the state's citizens found the institution
morally objectionable on racial grounds. The constitution also mandated that the descendents of slaves would remain in bondage in this
"free" state. Hence, the 1830 Illinois census listed 746 slaves.[3] Illinois
law allowed for slaves to enter the state and work on a temporary
basis, and a law passed in 1827 ordered stiff fines for anyone attempting to help them escape. Free blacks were required by law to carry a
freedom certificate with them at all times or face a fine or imprisonment. The white citizens of Illinois might have been generally opposed to slavery, but they certainly did not want free African
Americans in their midst, exercising their civil rights and, more prob-
lematically, competing with whites for jobs and undercutting the wage
scales.

It is not farfetched to speculate that the white citizens of Illinois in
Lincoln's time supported an antislavery state constitution not out of
sympathy for the plight of slaves or out of moral outrage over the institution of slavery but rather as a way of keeping black people out of the
state. Lincoln tried to score points using this line of reasoning with an
audience of Illinoisans at Peoria in 1854:

> In spite of the Ordinance of '87 [which prohibited slavery in Northwest
> Territory], a few negroes were brought into Illinois, and held in a state
> of quasi slavery; not enough, however, to carry a vote of the people in
> favor of the institution when they came to form a constitution. But in

the adjoining Missouri country, where there was no ordinance of '87—
was no restriction—they were carried ten times, nay a hundred times,
as fast, and actually made a slave State. That is fact—naked fact. (2:263)

Lincoln made the same point again during his 1858 campaign for the
Senate against Douglas, when he asserted that all United States territories should prohibit slavery so that they remain lands of opportunities for white people:

> I am still in favor of our new Territories being in such a condition that
> white men may find a home—may find some spot where they can better
> their condition—where they can settle upon new soil and better their
> condition in life. . . . I am in favor of this not merely . . . for our own
> people who are born amongst us, but as an outlet for *free white people
> everywhere,* the world over—in which Hans and Baptiste and Patrick,
> and all other men from all the world, may find new homes and better
> their conditions in life. (3:312)

In other words, if slavery is kept out of a state or territory, that region
will be free of African American settlers. It will remain the domain of
white people. That message would surely resonate with Illinois residents, who simply did not want black people living in their state. As
Garry Wills suggests, "Lincoln knew the racial geography of his own
state well, and calibrated what he had to say about slavery according
to his audience."[4]

Illinois was hardly unique among the free states in its racial attitudes during the first half of the nineteenth century. In 1837, state
legislators from southern Pennsylvania promoted a state constitutional convention for the primary purpose of passing an amendment
barring the immigration of African Americans into the state. (Thaddeus Stevens, a strong abolitionist voice in Pennsylvania politics,
blocked the move.) In 1847, an Ohio congressman warned that his
state's white citizens would line the Ohio River armed with muskets
to keep blacks out. On the state's books were so-called black laws and
black codes that limited the freedom of African Americans living in
Ohio. By 1860, only five states—all in New England—had extended
the right to vote to African American males. In the South, the belief

in the inferiority of blacks was articulated in the legislative halls, the newspapers, and the pulpit, but that belief was advanced not only in the South. As Leon F. Litwack states, "Although slavery eventually confined itself to the region below the Mason-Dixon Line, discrimination against the Negro and a firmly held belief in the superiority of the white race were not restricted to one section but were shared by an overwhelming majority of white Americans in both the North and the South," including Lincoln.[5]

Indeed, scholars have engaged in a vigorous debate over the extent to which Lincoln, during his pre-presidential political career, shared the racist views of so many Americans. Don E. Fehrenbacher suggests that Lincoln's opinions on race "were shaped more by his political realism than by impressions stamped on his mind in childhood." But Fehrenbacher sees a "doubleness in the man. . . . It appears that he may have both absorbed and doubted, both shared and risen above, the racial doctrines of his time."[6] Other scholars are less kind to Lincoln on this point. Richard Hofstadter asserts that "so far as the Negro was concerned, Lincoln could not escape the moral insensitivity that is characteristic of the average white American."[7] Mark E. Neely Jr. and Lerone Bennett Jr. concur.[8] Reinhold Niebuhr suggests that "Lincoln either shared the color prejudices of his and our day, or he was political enough not to challenge popular prejudices too radically."[9] David Zarefsky maintains that "Lincoln's racial thinking was enlightened" by the standards of his day, yet Zarefsky concedes that "it is easy for the twentieth-century reader of his speeches to find evidence of racism."[10]

Whether he absorbed the racist attitudes of his time and place or whether he developed his opinions on race through his own speculation, there is little doubt that, before his presidency, Lincoln, to a great degree, shared with the majority of his white countrymen and countrywomen a belief in the inferiority of African Americans and the superiority of the white race. Lincoln conveys this attitude in so many public and private utterances, over so long a period of time, that it is almost impossible to conclude otherwise. Lincoln's admirers will argue that his political career would have been stuck in quicksand had he not pandered, at least on occasion, to the racism of his electorate, and that might be true. Until he became president, however, Lincoln's views on issues of race were only slightly ahead of the attitude of the typical prejudiced white American.

Lincoln did embrace and articulate the belief that African Americans were human beings, included within the "created equal" clause of the Declaration of Independence—a conviction not widely held during the middle of the nineteenth century. Lincoln's antislavery position, which he began to exert with vigor in the summer of 1854, after the passage of the Kansas-Nebraska Act, was based on this conviction. In a speech in Bloomington, Illinois, delivered on September 26, 1854, Lincoln asserted his opposition to the Kansas-Nebraska Act because it opened United States territories to the institution of slavery; he maintained that the federal government had the right to prohibit slavery from expanding into the territories. If an African American is a human being, Lincoln argued in the Bloomington speech, then the federal government has no right to control the buying, selling, and transporting of African Americans, any more than the government has the right to regulate the oyster or cranberry trade, and "if the negro, upon soil where slavery is not legalized by law and sanctioned by custom, *is* a man, then there is not even the shadow of popular sovereignty in allowing the first settlers upon such soil to decide whether it shall be right in all future time to hold men in bondage there" (2:239). Lincoln made a similar point in a speech in Springfield, Illinois, the following week: "It is said that the slaveholder has the same [political] right to take his negroes to Kansas that a freeman has to take his hogs or his horses. This would be true if negroes were property in the same sense that hogs and horses are. But is this the case? It is notoriously not so" (2:245).

In his lengthy speech at Peoria, Illinois, in 1854, Lincoln hammered home the same themes. Again Lincoln defended the personhood of African Americans. "But if the negro *is* a man, is it not to that extent, a total destruction of self-government, to say that he too shall *not* govern *himself?*" he asked (2:266). For Lincoln, self-government involved people governing themselves; when they owned slaves, however, they exhibited not self-government but despotism. In Peoria, Lincoln also took up the question of whether the "created equal" clause of the Declaration of Independence of 1776 applied to African Americans. He reminded his audience that the nation's founding document had asserted the equality of all men, and he viewed slavery as a contradiction of that notion. Later in the speech, Lincoln declared, "Let us re-adopt the Declaration of Independence, and with it, the practices, and policy, which harmonize with it" (2:276).

Lincoln was troubled by the long-term implications of promulgating policies based on the notion that African Americans—or any group of people—were something less than human. If black Americans could be deemed inhuman or subhuman, then so could other minority groups within the United States. In a letter to his close friend Joshua Speed, written on August 24, 1855, Lincoln expressed this concern:

> Our progress in degeneracy appears to me to be pretty rapid. As a nation, we began by declaring that *"all men are created equal."* We now practically read it "all men are created equal, *except negroes."* When the Know-Nothings get control, it will read "all men are created equal, except negroes, *and foreigners, and catholics."* When it comes to this I should prefer emigrating to some country where they make no pretense of loving liberty—to Russia, for instance, where despotism can be taken pure, and without the base alloy of hypocrisy. (2:323)

If other American minorities were considered less than fully human— that is, created *unequal*—then slavery, theoretically at least, could spread to the white population. Here Lincoln might be accused of arguing on the slippery slope—except that, in the 1850s, Southerners like George Fitzhugh were claiming that slavery was the proper condition for both black and white laborers.[11]

By "created equal," however, Lincoln did not mean that all Americans would achieve complete equality in all aspects of life. He meant that every American, black and white, ought to be free to "make himself," as he expressed the idea in a speech at Kalamazoo, Michigan, in August 1856 (2:364). He believed that all Americans deserved the opportunity to rise, as Lincoln himself had done. "The man who labored for another last year, this year labors for himself, and next year he will hire others to labor for him," he explained at Kalamazoo (2:364). Lincoln believed that all Americans must have this opportunity to elevate themselves. The following year, in a letter to Theodore

Canisius, Lincoln put forth his belief that the spirit of American institutions is "to aim at the *elevation* of men"; he remained "opposed to whatever tends to *degrade* them" (3:380). Similarly, a fragment of a speech, probably composed in 1858 or 1859, states, "We proposed to give *all* a chance; and we expected the weak to grow stronger, the ignorant, wiser; and all better, and happier together" (2:222).

Lincoln elaborated on this argument in a speech at Springfield on June 26, 1857. Discussing a black woman, Lincoln stated, "In some respects she certainly is not my equal; but in her natural right to eat the bread she earns with her own hands without asking leave of any one else, she is my equal, and the equal of all others" (2:405). He continued:

> I think the authors of that ignoble instrument [the Declaration of Independence] intended to include *all* men, but they did not intend to declare all men equal *in all respects*. They did not mean to say all were equal in color, size, intellect, moral developments, or social capacity. They defined with tolerable distinctness, in what respects they did consider all men created equal—equal in "certain inalienable rights, among which are life, liberty, and the pursuit of happiness." (2:405–6)

Lincoln was not advancing the notion of a color-blind nation in which all Americans would be treated equally in all realms of society—social, political, legal, economic. He was saying that all Americans, including black people, have the fundamental right to eat the fruits of their labor and, through hard work, to improve their condition in life—a view not widely accepted in Illinois in the 1840s and 1850s.

In that Springfield address, Lincoln claimed that the "created equal" clause of the Declaration of Independence was a "standard maxim for a free society, . . . constantly labored for, and even though never perfectly attained, constantly approximated, and thereby constantly spreading and deepening its influence, and augmenting the happiness and value of life of all people of all colors everywhere" (2:406). Later in that speech, Lincoln rejected the idea that the Declaration of Independence applied only to the descendents of British subjects, a view articulated by Stephen Douglas; Lincoln argued that "the Declaration contemplated the progressive improvement in the condition of all

men everywhere" (2:407). He even believed that the spirit of the Declaration of Independence carries beyond the nation's boundaries; it applies to people over the whole world.

During his 1858 campaign for the Illinois Senate seat occupied by
Douglas, Lincoln held to that position, though it might not play well
with Illinois voters. In a campaign speech in Chicago, Lincoln asserted, "So I say in relation to the principle that all men are created
equal, let it be as nearly reached as we can. If we cannot give freedom
to every creature, let us do nothing that will impose slavery upon any
other creature" (2:501). Later in the speech, Lincoln made one of his
most progressive pre–Civil War statements on race relations in the
United States: "I have only to say, let us discard all this quibbling
about this man and the other man—this race and that race and the
other race being inferior, and therefore they must be placed in an inferior position. . . . Let us discard all these things, and unite as one people
throughout this land, until we shall once more stand up declaring that
all men are created equal" (2:501).

Lincoln continued to defend his inclusive view of the "created
equal" clause during his debates with Douglas. Indeed, he held fast to
that view through the beginning of his presidency. He articulated his
position on the Declaration of Independence in a speech in New
Haven, Connecticut, in March 1860, two months before he received
the Republican nomination for president, when he charged that *"the
whole Democratic party has deliberately taken negroes from the class
of men and put them in the class of brutes"* (4:19). Lincoln put forth a
similar defense of the Declaration of Independence in a fragment written in early 1861, as he was preparing for the presidency. He identified
the American commitment to "Liberty to all" as the main cause of the
nation's prosperity: "The *expression* of that principle, in our Declaration of Independence, was most happy, and fortunate. *Without* this, as
well as *with* it, we could have declared our independence of Great
Britain; but *without* it, we could not, I think, have secured our free
government, and consequent prosperity" (4:169).

Zarefsky suggests, however, that Lincoln's commitment to any specific plan to ensure equality for African Americans was minimal. Lincoln opposed slavery and included blacks in the "created equal" clause

of the Declaration of Independence, but, according to Zarefsky, Lincoln was "prepared to extend blacks no civil or political rights beyond freedom itself." This commitment "was the smallest departure from a position condoning slavery. It stopped short of any practical program . . . that might hasten the demise of slavery."[12] Lincoln's many statements on Negro suffrage and on the political and social equality of African Americans, uttered in public and private documents and oral statements during the first twenty-five years of his political career, provide disturbing evidence for Zarefsky's assessment.

During his first political campaign, for a seat in the Illinois legislature in 1836, Lincoln addressed the suffrage issue in a letter to the editor of the *Sangamo Journal*. "I go for all sharing the privileges of the government, who assist in bearing its burthens," he wrote. "Consequently I go for admitting all whites to the right of suffrage, who pay taxes or bear arms, (by no means excluding females.)" (1:48). Here Lincoln was advancing the concept that those who support the government by paying their tax bills or by enlisting in the militia deserve the right to determine the policies of the government via the ballot box. Lincoln included women, a progressive idea in 1836, when women could vote nowhere in the United States. But Lincoln was unwilling to apply this concept to African Americans, though they, too, might pay taxes into the state coffers. Lincoln's position on suffrage for blacks remained fixed through the early years of his presidency. In his first debate with Douglas during the Senate campaign of 1858, Lincoln stated, "I am not nor ever have been in favor of making voters or jurors of negroes" (3:145). In a speech in Columbus, Ohio, on September 16, 1859, Lincoln reiterated the view on black suffrage expressed in the 1858 debates. He would not change his view on this issue until African Americans began enlisting in the armed forces to fight in the Civil War.

In his important Peoria speech of October 16, 1854, Lincoln presented his most persuasive arguments against slavery and its extension into the United States territories, but he also conveyed to his audience his firm belief in the ideology of white supremacy. At Peoria, he confessed that he would not know what to do with the freed slaves if emancipation were immediately mandated. His first impulse would be to send the freed slaves to Liberia—"their own native land" (2:255)—though he realized that the execution of such a plan would be nearly impossible. Then Lincoln considered the prospect of freeing the slaves and allowing them the privileges of United States citizenship:

> Free them, and make them politically and socially, our equals? My own feelings will not admit of this; and if mine would, we well know that those of the great mass of white people will not. Whether this feeling accords with justice and sound judgment, is not the sole question, if indeed, it is any part of it. A universal feeling, whether well or ill-founded, can not be safely disregarded. We can not, then, make them our equals. (2:256)

Here Lincoln was revealing his own beliefs about the inferiority of the African American. He was also suggesting that, even if justice demanded equal treatment for African Americans, the prevailing attitudes on issues of race must be considered and acted upon.

During his debates with Douglas four years later, Lincoln continued to stand by the beliefs expressed in the Peoria address. Douglas, attempting to grab the political center of the Illinois electorate, tried to push Lincoln to the political extreme where abolitionists and civil rights advocates resided. Even before the debates, Douglas had been labeling Lincoln as a "Black Republican"—a Republican whose agenda advanced emancipation as well as the political, social, and economic equality of African Americans. Lincoln rejected the label and, in his first debate with Douglas, tried to distance himself from Black Republicanism:

> I have no purpose to introduce political and social equality between the white and black races. There is a physical difference between the two, which in my judgment will probably forever forbid their living together upon the footing of perfect equality, and inasmuch as it becomes a necessity that there must be a difference, I, as well as Judge Douglas, am in favor of the race to which I belong, having the superior position. I have never said anything to the contrary, but I hold that notwithstanding all this, there is no reason in the world why the negro is not entitled to all the natural rights enumerated in the Declaration of Independence, the right to life, liberty and the pursuit of happiness. I hold that he is as much entitled to these as the white man. (3:16)

Here a logical inconsistency in Lincoln's thinking is apparent, one that Douglas would exploit during future debates. Lincoln seemed to be simultaneously advocating white supremacy and equal rights for African Americans—at least the right to life (not to be exterminated), liberty (to move about freely and not to be held in bondage), and the pursuit of happiness (perhaps economic freedom, the freedom to improve one's condition to achieve a satisfactory life).

Perhaps sensing his contradiction, or sensing that he had gone too far in his defense of the black American's civil rights, Lincoln opened the second debate by endorsing the Fugitive Slave Law, rejecting the abolition of slavery in the District of Columbia, and declining support for a policy of prohibiting the addition of new slave states to the Union. But Douglas had already sensed an opening, one through which he could push Lincoln toward the Black Republican end of the political spectrum. Douglas, employing vicious race-baiting tactics, began speaking of one of his own recent speeches that was attended by Frederick Douglass. Douglass, according to Douglas, "reclined" with a white woman inside a carriage while the woman's husband "acted as driver" (3:55–56). Douglas then used the incident to attack Lincoln's views on race:

> All I have to say of it is this, that if you, Black Republicans, think that the negro ought to be on a social equality with your wives and daughters, and ride in a carriage with your wife, whilst you drive the team, you have a perfect right to do so. . . . I am told that one of Fred. Douglass' kinsmen, another rich black negro, is now traveling in this part of the State making speeches for his friend Lincoln as the champion of black men. . . . All I have to say on that subject is that those of you who believe that the negro is your equal and ought to be on an equality with you socially, politically, and legally; have a right to entertain those opinions, and of course will vote for Mr. Lincoln. (3:56)

Later in that debate, Douglas accused Lincoln of being completely "committed to this Black Republican platform" (3:65).

Douglas's charges in the second debate sent Lincoln reeling. Between the second and third debates, Lincoln tried to regain ground on the political center. In a speech at Carlinville, Lincoln rejected the abolitionist label and placed himself, on the slavery issue, alongside the late Henry Clay, the nationally popular Kentuckian who owned slaves yet, according to Lincoln, found slavery morally wrong and assumed its ultimate disappearance from American soil. Lincoln also rejected Douglas's charges concerning the issue of racial equality: "Douglas tries to make capital by charges of negro equality against me. My speeches have been printed and before the country for some time on this question, and Douglas knows the utter falsity of such a charge" (3:79). To prove his point, Lincoln read a section from his Peoria speech of 1854 that expressed his desire not to free the slaves and make them his equals. A week after the Carlinville speech, Lincoln made these same points in a speech at Bloomington.

But Douglas possessed a politician's sense for a winning argument. In the third debate, he again brought up the incident with Frederick Douglass riding in the carriage with the white woman while her husband drove. This time, Douglas described Douglass as "sitting inside with the white lady and her daughter" (3:105). Douglas was obviously playing to the unwarranted fears of white men in the audience who believed that black men wished to prey on white women. Douglas also noted that a man named John Dougherty supported Lincoln and that Dougherty's "allies at Chicago, advocated negro citizenship and negro equality, putting the white man and the negro on the same basis under the law" (3:106).

When Douglas tried to use these race-baiting tactics to push Lincoln to the political extreme, Lincoln, predictably, pushed back to regain the political center. He opened the fourth debate with his most forceful and detailed statement on the idea of racial equality:

> I will say then that I am not, nor ever have been in favor of bringing about in any way the social and political equality of the white and black races,—that I am not nor ever have been in favor of making voters or jurors of negroes, nor of qualifying them to hold office, nor to intermarry with white people; and I will say in addition to this that there is a physical difference between the white and black races which I believe will for ever forbid the two races living together on terms of social and political equality. And inasmuch as they cannot so live, while they do remain together there must be the position of superior and inferior, and I as

much as any other man am in favor of having the superior position assigned to the white race. (3:145–46)

Douglas pushed back; he charged that "Lincoln's ally, in the person of FRED. DOUGLASS, THE NEGRO," was preaching the same abolitionist doctrines as Lincoln advocated and that the Republicans had another "negro traversing the northern counties of the State, and speaking in behalf of Lincoln" (3:171). Lincoln responded by declaring that he is "not in favor of negro citizenship" (3:179).

Lincoln devoted much time during the final three debates to assuring his audiences that he was neither an abolitionist nor a proponent of equal rights for African Americans. In the fifth debate, however, Douglas exploited an obvious contradiction in Lincoln's views on race:

> Mr. Lincoln asserts to-day as he did at Chicago, that the negro was included in that clause of the Declaration of Independence which says that all men were created equal and endowed by the Creator with certain inalienable rights, among which are life, liberty and the pursuit of happiness. . . . If the negro was made his equal and mine, if that equality was established by Divine law, and was the negro's inalienable right, how came he to say at Charleston to the Kentuckians residing in that section of our State, that the negro was physically inferior to the white man, belonged to an inferior race, and he was for keeping him always in that inferior condition? (3:238)

Douglas then attacked Lincoln for geographic inconsistency—for advocating a certain level of equality for African Americans in speeches and debates that took place in Illinois's northern counties and for articulating white supremacy in the southern counties, where proslavery Kentuckians had migrated. But Douglas had also hit upon a logical contradiction as well. How could Lincoln suggest that African Americans were created equal and that they possessed the same inalienable rights as white people but that they should remain in an inferior social and political position in American society? Lincoln had no effective response to Douglas's inquiry, though, as LaWanda Cox suggests, Lincoln could not have been oblivious to the validity of Douglas's argument.[13] The purely logical response for Lincoln would be to endorse wholeheartedly the concept of racial equality, which Lincoln was unable to do at the time—for both political and philosophical reasons. He did not want to lose votes, and he did not believe, in 1858, that African Americans were his equals.

Lincoln's comments on race during the 1858 debates have troubled many Lincoln scholars. Some agree with Fehrenbacher that Lincoln's comments "grate harshly upon the modern ear" but that he had to make them for political reasons.[14] Oates, for example, suggests that Lincoln was forced to make white supremacist statements "or risk political ruin in white-supremacist Illinois."[15] Phillip Shaw Paludan argues that Lincoln backed away from a commitment to full racial equality for African Americans to avoid being compared to abolitionists like William Lloyd Garrison and John Brown, that "any politician who hoped for success in the mid-nineteenth-century United States could not embrace equality as an immediate truth."[16] Similarly, Zarefsky concludes that Lincoln's "political survival depended on avoiding the abolitionist label" by "disclaiming any support for Negro equality."[17] Benjamin Quarles is forgiving of Lincoln, claiming that "the jibes of his opponent forced him [Lincoln] to declare himself in opposition to Negro equality," that Lincoln was "a man without bigotry of any kind."[18] David Herbert Donald states that Lincoln's rejection of the idea of equality for African Americans was "a politically expedient thing to say" but that it "also expressed Lincoln's deeply held personal views, which he repeatedly expressed before."[19] Charles Strozier agrees that Lincoln made these racist statements not only to curry favor with Illinois voters but because "at this point in his life Lincoln was convinced blacks were inferior and did not deserve social or political equality with whites." According to Strozier, "it would be naïve to ignore the essential racism that informed Lincoln's thought wherever he spoke."[20]

Any honest assessment of Lincoln's racial views cannot easily excuse his comments during the debates with Douglas. Lincoln spoke extemporaneously during the heat of debate, but he had the opportunity to rethink his positions between debates, to back away from or clarify statements made in the early debates. Instead, Lincoln, as the debates progressed, seemed to distance himself further from the idea of racial equality; his anti–African American rhetoric gets stronger in the later debates. The argument that Lincoln was merely being politically shrewd during the debates, that he needed to reject the idea of racial equality to gain votes from an electorate that was hardly progressive on racial issues, has merit. An Illinois politician might not go far in 1858 by embracing the abolitionist cause and by advocating complete equality for African Americans. Yet there can be little doubt, as Donald suggests, that Lincoln, politics aside, for the most part, embraced the racist views of many white Americans during the mid-nineteenth century.

A legitimate question to ask is whether Lincoln should be held, on issues of race, to the standards of our time rather than to those of his own era, by which Lincoln, as Zarefsky suggests, would probably be judged as racially enlightened. Surely today's electorate would bury a politician who expressed an ideology of white supremacy, so why should we excuse Lincoln? According to Oates, however, "We learn nothing at all, if his [Lincoln's] words are lifted from their historical setting and judged only by the standards of another time."[21] Do we have the right to hold historical figures to the standards of our own times? Eric Foner recently responded to that question in a letter to the editor of the *New York Times*. "Historians are taught not to judge the past by present standards," he wrote. "It would be wrong, for example, to criticize Lincoln for not speaking out in favor of gay rights, which was not part of the public discussion then."[22] To fault Lincoln for not speaking out on gay rights would be as unfair, perhaps, as criticizing Civil War physicians for not using penicillin to fight infection or for not administering blood transfusions to save lives on the battlefield.

The ideas about racial equality that we advance today, however, were certainly part of the public discourse during Lincoln's time, though those ideas were not widely embraced. William Lloyd Garrison, Wendell Phillips, Theodore Weld, Frederick Douglass, Theodore Parker, Sarah and Angelina Grimké, and others in the abolitionist vanguard endorsed racial equality for all Americans. Surely Lincoln was familiar with their speeches and writings; the idea that African Americans should enjoy the civil rights guaranteed to other Americans was not completely foreign to Lincoln.[23] And advocating the civil rights of African Americans did not necessarily mean, in 1858, sacrificing a political career. William Seward of New York, the favorite to gain the Republican Party's presidential nomination in 1860, was a strong proponent of civil rights for African Americans. So was Thaddeus Stevens of the border state of Pennsylvania. Lincoln might have survived politically had he refused to articulate so passionately the view that African Americans were inferior to whites and did not deserve the rights enjoyed by white Americans.

Oates is correct when he states that Lincoln, before the Civil War, "did not envision black people as permanent participants in the great American experiment."[24] Conversely, Lincoln saw their presence on American soil as a problem—one that was dividing the nation and threatening the Union. Lincoln's solution to this problem was to endorse the mission of the American Colonization Society, a mission that many African American leaders found distasteful.[25] The American Colonization Society, which was founded in 1816 and secured federal funding in 1819, sought to encourage the emigration of African Americans to Africa and, later, South America. In 1822, the society established Liberia, on the west coast of Africa, as a country to which free African Americans could migrate. Between 1822 and the start of the Civil War, about twelve thousand African Americans left the United States and settled in Liberia.

The organization gained the support of many white Americans, including some abolitionists. In 1829, Garrison declared himself a colonizationist, but he announced a change of heart in the first edition of the *Liberator* in 1831. Henry Highland Garnet, an African American abolitionist, backed colonization because he believed that African Americans would never achieve equality in the United States. Lyman Beecher, the father of Harriet Beecher Stowe, also endorsed colonization, and his daughter supported colonization as well. In the final chapters of *Uncle Tom's Cabin*, George and Eliza Harris, the escaped slaves, find their way to Liberia. In the novel's concluding chapter, a lecture by the author on the evils of slavery, Stowe recommends the exportation of freed slaves to Liberia, after they have received "the educating advantages of Christian republican society and schools."[26] Lincoln's political role model, Henry Clay, also backed colonization.

Lincoln first articulated his support for colonization in his eulogy on Clay, delivered on July 6, 1852. In that speech, Lincoln quoted Clay on the merits of sending African Americans to Africa and then advocated colonization himself: "This [Clay's] suggestion of the possible ultimate redemption of the African race and African continent, was made twenty-five years ago. Every succeeding year has added strength to the hope of its realization. May it indeed be realized!" (2:132). Lincoln added that if America could "succeed in freeing our land from the dangerous presence of slavery; and, at the same time, in restoring a captive people to their long-lost father-land, . . . it will indeed be a glorious consummation" (2:132).

Lincoln made the same point in his speech at Peoria two years later, when he asserted that his solution to the problems caused by slavery would be to free American slaves and allow them to emigrate to Liberia. (By the time of the Civil War, however, only 1 percent of American slaves were born abroad.)[27] Three years later, in a speech at Springfield, Lincoln warned of the dangers of miscegenation—"the mixing of blood in the nation" (2:409); he noted the widespread sexual exploitation of female slaves by their white masters. He then declared that "the separation of the races is the only perfect preventative of amalgamation. . . . Such separation, if ever effected at all, must be effected by colonization" (2:409). Lincoln would continue to support various colonization schemes until halfway through the Civil War.

Lincoln advocated colonization for three reasons. First, he saw it as a solution to the problems caused by slavery. Slavery, in Lincoln's view, developed in America because of the presence of black people; if black people could be removed gradually from American soil, slavery would die a natural death. Second, Lincoln, by the late 1850s, had come to believe, along with many other colonization supporters, that African Americans would never obtain their civil rights on United States soil; they would remain in a position of social, political, legal, and economic inferiority forever. Lincoln honestly believed African Americans would be more likely to prosper in a country of their own than in the United States. Third, Lincoln, in the late 1850s, shared with many other white Americans a preference for living in a segregated society—a society inhabited by white people. "What I would most desire would be the separation of the white and black races," he said in a speech in Springfield on July 17, 1858 (2:521). The most effective way of separating the races, in Lincoln's view, would be to send African Americans to another continent across the sea.

Neely calls the plan for colonization "a profoundly racist dream, rooted in an inability to imagine a biracial future for America if the black race were free, and wholly unrealistic."[28] It might have been a dream solution to America's racial problems in the mid-nineteenth century, but implementing the plan would have been a nightmare. The idea of shipping four or five million African Americans across the sea to Africa was, of course, preposterous; the logistics of implementing such a plan were mind-boggling. The costs would be astronomical. Lincoln scholars have found Lincoln's support for it baffling. "For a man who prided himself on his rationality, his adherence to such an unworkable scheme was puzzling," states Donald. But Donald offers an explanation: "Lincoln's persistent advocacy of colonization served an unconscious purpose of preventing him from thinking too much about a problem [slavery] that he found insoluble."[29] Paludan claims that colonization was, in Lincoln's mind, a placebo to calm the concerns of whites who feared immediate emancipation.[30] White Americans might more readily accept emancipation if they knew that freed blacks would be leaving the country.

Perhaps, as Donald and Paludan suggest, Lincoln needed to believe in some solution to the problems posed by slavery, and he embraced colonization as the most reasonable solution at hand. It was, however, unworkable on anything grander than a minimal scale. Several thousand African Americans might consent to leave the United States for better prospects in Africa, Haiti, or South America, but how could the federal government entice four or five million to emigrate and then finance their transportation? Moreover, as Neely suggests, the plan was rooted in racism. As Frederick Douglass and other African American opponents of colonization pointed out, the overwhelming majority of blacks living in the United States during the 1850s, slaves and freemen, were born on American soil; the families of many had been living in the New World for several generations. They were Americans, not Africans. But Lincoln, in the 1850s, was still unable to see

African Americans as his fellow citizens; he preferred that they leave America to white people. Lerone Bennett Jr. is on the mark when he states that Lincoln "considered black people unassimible aliens. There was not, in his view, enough room in America for black and white people."[31] Lincoln would continue to propose this racist solution to America's racial problem until the middle of the Civil War, when African American soldiers began enlisting in the Union army.

Strozier finds additional evidence for Lincoln's racist thinking in the imagery that he often used to describe slaves and African Americans. In his writings and speeches before the Civil War, Lincoln compared slaves to fish, hogs, ants, and other "creatures."[32] For example, in his letter to Mary Speed, written in 1841, Lincoln described slaves chained together aboard a riverboat as "fish upon a trot-line"; they are, nonetheless, "the most cheerful and happy creatures on board" (1:260). In an editorial in the *Illinois Journal*, published in 1854, Lincoln compared the opening of free territory to slavery to the opening of a fenced luscious pasture to starving cattle. The slaves are the cattle (2:230). In an 1855 letter to Joshua Speed, Lincoln explained that he felt sorry for runaway slaves who were captured and returned to bondage: "I confess I hate to see the poor creatures hunted down, and caught, and carried back to their stripes, and unrewarded toils" (2:320). Strozier states that this animal imagery "seemed to suppress the agonizing human experience of the slaves he saw. To compare the slaves with fish on a trotline was to see them as objects."[33] Despite Lincoln's assertions that African Americans are human beings included in the "created equal" clause of the Declaration of Independence, his imagery suggests that he saw them as "creatures" that were something less than fully human.

Also troubling, at least to the modern reader, is Lincoln's use of the word "nigger." The term sounded almost as unpleasant to African Americans in the mid-nineteenth century as it does today, and Lincoln used it, at least on occasion.[34] Lincoln employed the word in his last debate with Douglas in 1858, when he stated, "There is no danger that the people of Kentucky will shoulder their muskets and with a young nigger stuck on every bayonet march into Illinois and force them upon us" (3:27). Ironically, he used the term in a speech at Hartford in 1860 in which he attacked slavery as a moral wrong. Early in the speech,

Lincoln, in less-than-clear language, criticized the nation for becoming indifferent about slavery:

> Some men think it is a question of neither right or wrong; that it is a question of dollars and cents, only; that the Almighty has drawn a line across the country, south of which the land is always to be cultivated by slave labor; when the question is between the white man and the nigger, they go in for the white man; when it is between the nigger and the crocodile, they take sides with the nigger. There is effort to make the feeling of indifference prevalent in the country, and this is one of those things, perhaps, that prevents the sudden settlement of the question. (4:4)

Lincoln did not use "nigger" too often in his speeches or writings; he usually referred to African Americans as Negroes or black people. But his use of the word in public, even on occasion, suggests, minimally, racial insensitivity.

Lincoln carried these views on race into the White House in 1861. Before and after the presidential election of 1860, he continued to hold fast to his position of keeping slavery from gaining a toehold in the United States territories, but he backed away from the abolitionists. He criticized John Brown; he pledged not to interfere with slavery in the states in which it already existed. In a letter written a month after the election, Lincoln assured Henry J. Raymond, the editor of the *New York Times*, that he "is not pledged to the ultimate extinction of slavery" and "does not hold the black man to be the equal of the white" (4:156). On December 20, 1860, Lincoln penned for a Republican committee working on the slavery issue a resolution endorsing strict enforcement of the Fugitive Slave Law (4:156).

Lincoln's First Inaugural Address was an appeal for the status quo. He assured the South that his administration would not threaten the region's human property: "I only press upon the public attention the most conclusive evidence of which the case is susceptible, that the property, peace and security of no section are to be in anywise endangered by the now incoming Administration" (4:263). He asserted the constitutional basis for the Fugitive Slave Law. He made no statement that suggested a change in the nation's racial situation. Quarles reports that African Americans were disappointed by the address.[35] Lincoln, on March 4, 1861, was interested in preserving the Union, not in defending the humanity or rights of African Americans. He would not begin to reassess his opinions on race until two years later, when the turmoil and tragedy of civil war shook the foundations of his thinking.

THREE

Lincoln's Religion:
"The Doctrine of Necessity"

DURING ABRAHAM LINCOLN'S CAMPAIGN for a seat in the House of Representatives in 1846, his opponent, Peter Cartwright, began circulating the rumor that Lincoln was an infidel. In the mid-nineteenth century, a charge of religious infidelity, if it stuck, would certainly have spelled political ruin for any candidate, so Lincoln moved quickly to dismiss Cartwright's accusation. On July 31, a few days before the election, Lincoln distributed a carefully worded handbill denying his opponent's charge and explaining his own religious beliefs. (After the election, the handbill was printed in local newspapers.) "That I am not a member of any Christian Church, is true," the handbill stated; "but I have never denied the truth of the Scriptures; and I have never spoken with intentional disrespect of religion in general, or of any denomination of Christians in particular." Lincoln added that "early in life I was inclined to believe in what I understand is called the 'Doctrine of Necessity'—that is, that the human mind is impelled to action, or held in rest by some power, over which the mind has no control. . . . I have always understood this same opinion to be held by several of the Christian denominations." Lincoln concluded the document by stating that he probably could not support any candidate for public office whom he knew to be "an open enemy of, and scoffer at, religion" and by blaming those "who falsely put such a charge in circulation" against him (1:382).

Allen C. Guelzo correctly states that Lincoln's 1846 handbill "allowed Lincoln to deny having any open hostility to Christianity without actually affirming any preference for it."[1] Lincoln stated that he never denied the truth of the Scriptures, but he did not claim that he believed in the truth of the Scriptures. He asserted that he never spoke with disrespect toward religion in general or toward any particular religious sect, but he did not claim to be a follower of any religion either. He openly admitted that he had not joined any church. Although Lincoln acknowledged a belief in the Doctrine of Necessity, he did not elaborate on that conviction. In short, Lincoln denied being a religious scoffer without really committing himself to any creed.

Perhaps Lincoln, in this handbill, was playing the role of the consummate politician who is unwilling to reveal any deep religious personal belief that could alienate a segment of the electorate. Had he identified himself as a Baptist, the Methodists might have deserted his campaign. Had he spelled out his religious beliefs more clearly, he might have alienated voters who did not profess the same beliefs. If Lincoln was being intentionally ambiguous to garner votes—or to prevent the loss of votes during the final days of the election campaign—then his strategy was successful: Lincoln easily defeated Cartwright, 6,340 votes to 4,829.[2] The handbill, however, reveals more than Lincoln's political skills; it provides some insight into his religious beliefs in 1846. Lincoln, at the age of thirty-seven, had not yet comfortably settled upon a specific religious creed or core of religious beliefs. As he approached middle age, Lincoln, in matters of faith, was still exploring.

Lincoln had grown up in a religious family. His parents were Separate Baptists, distinguished from other Baptists by their exclusive dependence on the Bible in matters of faith (as opposed to Regular Baptists who accepted the Philadelphia Confession of Faith). In many important ways, the religious beliefs of the Separate Baptists mirrored those of the Puritans and Calvinists who came to America in the seventeenth century and whose influence was still widely felt in Lincoln's time. The Separate Baptists inherited from Calvinism the doctrine of predestination, the belief that an all-powerful God controlled the universe and determined the fate of human beings in this world and the next. The Puritan God superintended the lives of both individuals and the fate of peoples and nations, and this God exacted harsh retribution on those who disobeyed him. The Puritan poet Anne Bradstreet demonstrated this belief in God's careful supervision of the lives of individuals in a section of a letter to her children, written a few years before her death in 1672:

> But as I grew to be about 14 or 15, I found my heart more carnal, and sitting loose from God, vanity and the follies of youth take hold of me.
> About 16, the Lord laid His hand sore upon me and smote me with the smallpox. When I was in my affliction, I besought the Lord and confessed my pride and vanity, and He was entreated of me and again restored me.[3]

The teenage Bradstreet sinned—her heart became "more carnal"—and God administered a severe punishment: a case of smallpox, a disease that was often fatal during the seventeenth century. When Bradstreet confessed her sins, however, the Lord intervened to help her recover. As a child, Lincoln undoubtedly learned at home and in church of a God who reacted to sin with similarly stiff reprimands.

One of the most popular Puritan texts was *The Narrative of the Captivity and Restoration of Mrs. Mary Rowlandson*, which demonstrates the Puritan belief that God also controls the fate of nations and peoples. First published in 1682, Rowlandson's widely read narrative remained in print throughout the colonial period and into the nineteenth century. Rowlandson's text is both a lively adventure narrative—the story of her twelve-week captivity by the Wampanoag Indians of southeastern Massachusetts during King Philip's War—and a Puritan morality tale that vividly portrays the Puritan God. Rowlandson does not dwell on the political tensions that led to the war between the Wampanoags and the English settlers; for her, the war is God's punishment upon the Massachusetts colony for turning away from him. During her captivity, Rowlandson observes God's hand in every action. He silences the dogs guarding the English settlement so that the Wampanoags can enter unimpeded and torment the settlers. The Wampanoags successfully cross the Baquag River with their hostages, but the Lord renders the waterway impassable to the pursuing

British, thus "preserving the heathen for farther affliction to our poor country."[4] When a Wampanoag man gives Rowlandson a Bible taken from an English village during a raid, Rowlandson sees the gesture as an act of mercy from God to provide her with strength during her captivity. Upon her release—Rowlandson is eventually ransomed by the English—she views her ordeal as God's resolution to scourge and chasten her and her people for failing to place all of their trust in him.

The Puritan God whom Lincoln came to know in his youth was that stern judge who exacted severe punishment on those who disobeyed him. Lincoln's God was the vengeful Supreme Being of Jonathan Edwards's quintessentially Puritan 1741 sermon, "Sinners in the Hands of an Angry God":

> The bow of God's wrath is bent, and the arrow made ready on the string, and justice bends the arrow at your heart, and strains the bow, and it is nothing but the mere pleasure of God, and that of an angry God, without any promise or obligation at all, that keeps the arrow one moment from being made drunk with your blood. Thus all you that never passed under a great change of heart, by the mighty power of the Spirit of God upon your souls; all you that were never born again, and made new creatures, and raised from being dead in sin, to a state of new, and before altogether unexperienced light and life, are in the hands of an angry God.[5]

The Puritans saw human beings as depraved individuals, prone to sin, who deserved God's wrath and punishment.

Though the Puritans' influence on American culture had weakened somewhat during the decades after Edwards delivered his potent jeremiad, their vengeful Supreme Being survived into the mid-nineteenth century. As Edmund Wilson points out, "Though Calvinism was being displaced by more liberal forms of religion—Unitarianism in New England dates from 1820—the old fierceness, the old Scriptural assertiveness of the founders of the New England theocracy had not yet been wholly tamed by their children."[6] The religious principles of American Calvinism were, in Lincoln's day, widely embraced. The preachers associated with the Second Great Awakening might have challenged some of the rigid Calvinist principles, such as the belief in predestination, but the new generation of clergymen still emphasized the need for individuals to acknowledge their failings, to repent their sins, and to reform and thus save themselves from God's wrath. Countless believers of Lincoln's time still saw human beings as sinners in the hands of an angry God.

Many on the abolitionist vanguard absorbed the Puritan principles and translated them into a vigorous religious attack on the institution of slavery. For abolitionists, slavery was a national sin, a very public stain of immorality on the garb of the American republic. Slavery was also a grievous offense against God, one that would eventually result in God's most severe retribution. David Walker sounded this theme in his 1829 abolitionist tract, *Walker's Appeal in Four Articles.* "I tell you Americans! that unless you speedily alter your course, *you* and your Country are gone!!!!!" wrote Walker. "For God Almighty will tear up the very face of the earth!!! . . . This language, perhaps, is too harsh for the American's delicate ears. But O Americans! Americans!! I warn you in the name of the Lord . . . to repent and reform, or you are ruined!!!"[7] More than two decades later, Harriet Beecher Stowe concluded *Uncle Tom's Cabin* with a similar message:

> A day of grace is yet held out to us. Both North and South have been guilty before God; and the *Christian church* has a heavy account to answer. Not by combining together, to protect injustice and cruelty, and making a common capital of sin, is this Union to be saved,—but by repentance, justice, and mercy; for, not surer is the eternal law by which the millstone sinks in the ocean, than that stronger law, by which injustice and cruelty shall bring on nations the wrath of Almighty God![8]

Louis A. Warren reports that the two ministers of the Indiana church that Lincoln attended as a child were ardent abolitionists. Warren surmises that some of the first sermons that young Lincoln heard were on the evils of slavery.[9] In his adulthood, Lincoln never fully embraced the abolitionist cause, yet Edmund Wilson sees a connection between Lincoln's condemnation of slavery on moral grounds and "the spirit of the New England crusaders who were to turn the conflict of interests between the Northern and Southern states into a Holy War led by God."[10] William J. Wolf argues that Lincoln's opposition to slavery was primarily moral, rather than economic or political, and that Lincoln's "conception of morality itself was derived from religion."[11]

As a young man, however, Lincoln distanced himself from his parents' religion. Lincoln's father, Thomas Lincoln, was one of the founders of the Pigeon Creek Baptist Church in Indiana, but Lincoln never joined that church or any other (though he did, during periods of his life, attend Sunday services and even rented pews in churches in Springfield, Illinois, and in Washington). Wolf suggests that Lincoln chose not to join any particular church or sect because he was repelled by the intense rivalries among Baptists, Methodists, and other sects on the American frontier where he grew into adulthood.[12] That might be so, but an equally plausible explanation for Lincoln's lack of religious affiliation is that he had become, in his early adulthood, a Victorian doubter, a brooder on matters of faith who would not easily settle on any definite set of religious principles. Even at an early age, he lived the examined life; he engaged in constant speculation about religious matters rather than accepting a set of creeds put forth by a specific religious sect.

Lincoln separated from his family for good in 1831, at age twenty-two, when he moved to the village of New Salem, Illinois, where he lived for six years before relocating to Springfield. According to Douglas L. Wilson, Lincoln, during his years in New Salem, associated with a group of young men who had the reputation of being freethinking scoffers and skeptics on matters of faith.[13] These young men frequently engaged in religious debate, and they introduced Lincoln to the writings of Thomas Paine and Constantin de Volney. Paine believed in God, but he deeply mistrusted religious institutions, preferring instead a personal creed that stressed justice for all and love of neighbor. Volney emphasized natural reason as an alternative to what he considered the arbitrary opinions of specific religions. Wilson states that Lincoln never claimed to be an atheist but was, as a young man, "so strongly critical of orthodox Christian beliefs that he sometimes looked like one to his more conventional friends."[14]

Lincoln's reputation apparently followed him to Springfield, as the charge of religious infidelity by Peter Cartwright during the congressional campaign of 1846 suggests. Wolf offers plausible reasons to explain why Cartwright's charge might have stuck. First, Wolf points out that the word "infidel" was used quite loosely in the mid-nineteenth century. A person who believed that the earth revolved around the sun would be labeled an infidel, as would anyone who questioned any aspect of the Scriptures. A person belonging to a religious sect out of the mainstream might also be charged with religious infidelity. Second, Lincoln, by this time, had developed some unorthodox religious beliefs. For example, he had come to believe in universal salvation, a religious principle that would have been judged as heresy by believers in the Calvinistic notion of eternal damnation for sinners.[15] Moreover, by not becoming a member of any church, Lincoln might have raised the suspicions of the many churchgoers among his electorate.

Elton Trueblood is probably correct when he states that Lincoln "felt at home in the Illinois legislature as he never did in any Illinois church."[16] Lincoln stepped away from his parents' faith; he did not join any church; he associated with religious skeptics; and he, like many other intellectuals of the Victorian era, brooded over religious matters rather than accepting the prepackaged creeds of any religious sect. He entered middle age still speculating in matters of faith. Nonetheless, the Puritanical beliefs of Lincoln's parents, which were still strongly evident in American culture in the mid-nineteenth century, took hold in him in important ways during his early adult years and remained with him through middle age. For comparison, consider James Baldwin, the twentieth-century African American writer. Baldwin grew up in the Christian church. His father was a self-ordained minister, and by the age of fourteen, the younger Baldwin was delivering sermons in Harlem's storefront churches. At age sixteen or seventeen, however, Baldwin broke from the church. He never returned to it in a formal way, but Christian motifs and the Christian message permeate his best literary efforts—*Go Tell It on the Mountain, The Fire Next Time,* "Sonny's Blues."

Douglas L. Wilson states that Lincoln "seems to have resisted most of the religious beliefs of his parents, [but] he retained throughout life a fatalism that one may believe was fostered in part by the Calvinist bent of his Baptist upbringing."[17] Indeed, more than one Lincoln scholar has connected Lincoln's belief in the Doctrine of Necessity to the Calvinist notion of predestination. In the 1846 handbill distributed in response to Cartwright's charge of religious infidelity, Lincoln defined the Doctrine of Necessity as the belief that "the human mind is impelled to action, or held in rest by some power over which the mind itself has no control" (1:382). To espouse the Doctrine of Necessity is to believe in fatalism or determinism—to believe that human beings have little control over their actions or destiny, that a divine power or the forces of nature predetermine human events. Wilson sees Lincoln's fatalism as "an outgrowth of the Calvinistic religious worldview in which he was raised. . . . [H]e retained the fatalistic premise at its core: that man does not control his own destiny."[18] Similarly, David Herbert Donald states that Lincoln, from his earliest days, "had a sense that his destiny was controlled by some larger force, some Higher Power." As a result, Lincoln, as a young man, embraced the Doctrine of Necessity.[19]

In conflict with the Doctrine of Necessity, however, was Lincoln's receptiveness to the rationalism of the Enlightenment. In his address at the Young Men's Lyceum in 1838, his most significant speech to this point in his political career, Lincoln stressed the importance of reason, rather than passion, in solving the nation's problems: "Passion has helped us; but can do so no more. It will in future be our enemy. Reason, cold, calculating, unimpassioned reason, must furnish all the materials for our future support and defense" (1:115). To embrace both the notion of fatality and the belief that human beings could use their sense of reason to choose the best course of action to shape their destinies was to embrace a contradiction. Wolf maintains that "the inconsistency here is a real one and Lincoln never clearly resolved the issue philosophically."[20] Indeed, both a belief in fatality and a faith in reason are evident in Lincoln's writings and speeches. This contradiction at the core of Lincoln's system of beliefs reveals that he was, in 1846, still struggling with religious issues.

Wolf suggests that the direction of Lincoln's religious fatalism after the publication of the 1846 handbill was "toward a deeper understanding of the biblical stress upon God's will and upon his own responsibility as 'God's instrument.'"[21] The notion of being an instrument in God's hand is evident in two of Lincoln's earliest surviving written comments on religious matters, two letters to Joshua Speed penned on February 8 and July 4, 1842. Speed's fiancée, Fanny Henning, had taken ill, and Speed worried that his marriage to her might result in great pain if she were to die. Shortly before the wedding, he wrote to his friend Lincoln about the matter, and Lincoln responded with sound advice. Lincoln noted that Speed had sometimes confessed doubts about his affection for Henning. In Lincoln's view, Speed's current anxiety about Henning's health "will forever banish those horrid doubts" (1:267). Lincoln then stated that he felt "a presentiment that the Almighty has sent your present affliction expressly for that object"—to remove Speed's doubts about his affection for Henning (1:267). Lincoln advised Speed to "rejoice, and not sorrow, at this indubitable evidence of your undying affection for her" (1:268).

Speed apparently accepted his good friend's advice; he married Henning several days later. A few months afterward, Speed wrote to Lincoln to inform him of his marital happiness and to thank him for the advice that he had provided in Speed's moments of doubt over the union. Lincoln's response to Speed's gratitude reveals much about Lincoln's view of God and his own role as an instrument of God:

> You make a kind acknowledgement of your obligations to me for your present happiness. I am much pleased with that acknowledgement; but a thousand times more am I pleased to know, that you enjoy a degree of happiness, worth of an acknowledgement. The truth is, I am not sure there was any merit, with me, in the part I took in your difficulty; I was drawn to it as by fate; if I would, I could not have done less than I did. I always was superstitious; and as part of my superstition, I believe God made me one of the instruments of bringing your Fanny and you together, which union, I have no doubt He fore-ordained. Whatever he designs, he will do for *me* yet. "Stand *still* and see the salvation of the Lord" is my text just now. (1:289)

Here, in these two letters to Speed, Lincoln revealed his fatalism—his belief that God has a design for each human being and that God manipulates worldly events to achieve that design. As Lincoln saw it, God inflicted illness upon Fanny Henning as a device to prompt Speed into realizing his love for her. God then sent Lincoln to Speed as an interpreter, to reveal to Speed the meaning of the illness that God visited upon Henning. Hence, Lincoln became God's instrument to guarantee that the marriage between Joshua Speed and Fanny Henning would take place. And Lincoln also suggested that God had some specific design for Lincoln in the future.

Lincoln put forth the same idea in a letter to his stepbrother, John D. Johnston, several years later, on January 12, 1851. The letter was occasioned by Lincoln's father's illness. Johnston had asked Lincoln to visit his father because the old man was gravely ill, perhaps near death. (Thomas Lincoln died on January 17, 1851.) Lincoln stated in the letter that he was too involved with business affairs to visit. He recommended securing the services of a doctor to treat his father; then he offered some advice: "[T]ell him to remember to call upon, and confide in, our great, and good, and merciful Maker; who will not turn away from him in any extremity. He notes the fall of a sparrow, and numbers the hairs of our heads; and he will not forget the dying man, who puts his trust in Him" (2:97).

If God controls the fate of relatively unimportant events like the marriage between two people, if he is aware of a sparrow's fall, then surely, in Lincoln's mind, God oversees and directs world events that have a substantial impact on humankind. Lincoln certainly believed this notion to be true. Thus, he could state with confidence, in his fourth debate with Stephen Douglas during the 1858 Senate campaign, that the abolition of slavery "will occur in the best way for both races in God's own good time" (3:181). In Lincoln's view, God planned to rid the United States of slavery but would not do so until he deemed that the time was right, for both races. Then, presumably, God would use human beings as his instruments to rid America of slavery; in his own good time, God would guide people's actions to achieve his plan of abolishing slavery in the United States.

Lincoln would come to believe firmly that God had a design for the United States; specifically, God had a plan to deal with the slavery issue. The great difficulty, Lincoln was beginning to realize during the 1850s as the slavery debate divided the nation, was to discover God's plan, to determine God's will. Southerners, too, believed that God had a plan for the nation. In their view, God had allowed slavery to take root on American soil in 1619. God had guided the authors of the Constitution as they established the American republic and drafted a document that protected slavery. Could God not have used Chief Justice Roger Taney as an instrument to extend slavery by directing Taney's decision in the case of *Dred Scott*? Perhaps, as many Southern clergymen maintained, God had deemed slavery the proper condition for black people. Lincoln articulated this problem in a speech in Chicago on March 1, 1859:

> Suppose it is true that the Almighty has drawn a line across this continent, on the south side of which part of the people will hold the rest as slaves; that the Almighty ordered this; that it is right, unchangeably right, that men ought there to be held as slaves, and that their fellow men will always have the right to hold them as slaves. I ask you, this once admitted, how can you believe that it is not right for us, or for them coming here, to hold slaves on this other side of the line? Once we come to acknowledge that it is right, that it is the law of the Eternal Being, for slavery to exist on one side of the line, have we any sure ground to object to slaves being held on the other side? Once admit the position that a man rightfully holds another man as property on one side of the line, and you must, when it suits his convenience to come to the other side, admit that he has the same right to hold property there. (3:368–69)

By this time, Lincoln had already argued, in various venues, that slavery was immoral. How, then, can God—who, in Lincoln's view, surely had a plan for the abolition of slavery in the United States—allow slavery to continue, perhaps spread, and the nation divide? Lincoln would dwell on this question for the next several years, until he resolved it during the crucible of the Civil War.

By 1859, however, Lincoln was taking the position in his public addresses that slavery was a great evil that would bring upon the nation the wrath of God. He was beginning to sound like the fire-and-brimstone Puritan preachers of his youth, scolding their congregations for their collective sins and predicting that God's wrath would soon come down upon the community. During the spring of 1859, Lincoln received an invitation to attend a festival in Boston commemorating the birthday of Thomas Jefferson. Lincoln wrote to the festival's organizers to say that he could not attend, but he used the letter to make a few remarks about Jefferson and slavery. (The letter was subsequently printed in Republican newspapers around the nation.) Lincoln praised Jefferson for his commitment to people's personal rights over their property rights. He lamented that, in the view of many of his fellow citizens, "the *liberty* of one man [is] to be absolutely nothing, when in conflict with another man's right of *property*" (3:375). Lincoln went on to write that they lived in "a world of compensations; and he who would *be* no slave, must consent to *have* no slave. Those who deny freedom to others, deserve it not for themselves; and, under a just God, can not long retain it" (3:376).

For the first time, in this 1859 letter, Lincoln identified slavery as a grievous sin that would be punished eventually by a just God. For five years, Lincoln had been calling slavery a moral wrong, but in this letter, he went beyond a moral condemnation of the institution of slavery. Here Lincoln suggested that slavery was against God's plan for the nation, that a just God would some day deprive slaveholders of their own freedom. This letter contains the seed for the more profound articulation of the same idea in Lincoln's Second Inaugural Address. Lincoln had begun to sense that God was displeased with the nation for its tolerance of slavery and that God would, in his own time and way, make the nation pay for its sin. An angry God would eventually punish Americans for their offenses.

Lincoln expressed the same idea several months later in a lengthy speech at Columbus, Ohio. In this address, Lincoln sounded familiar themes on the slavery issue—his concern over the extension of slavery into the territories, his criticism of the *Dred Scott* decision, his opposition to the idea of popular sovereignty championed by Stephen Douglas. At one point in the speech, Lincoln told his audience that Douglas ought to remember one of Jefferson's most quoted statements about slavery: "I tremble for my country when I remember that God is just!" (3:410). Then Lincoln, like a Puritan preacher explicating the biblical text selected for his sermon, clarified Jefferson's statement:

We know how he [Jefferson] looked upon it when he thus expressed himself. There was danger to this country—danger of the avenging justice of

God. . . . He supposed there was a question of God's eternal justice wrapped up in the enslaving of any race of men, or any man, and that those who did so braved the arm of Jehovah—that when a nation thus dared the Almighty every friend of that nation had cause to dread His wrath. Choose ye between Jefferson and Douglas as to what is the true view of this element among us. (3:410)

In this statement, Lincoln unequivocally asserted that God was angry with the nation for its involvement with slavery. Jefferson, too, had sensed it many years earlier, yet the nation continued to tolerate slavery on its soil. Lincoln was beginning to sense that such complacency over a moral wrong would soon result in God's wrath.

This comment about Jefferson, slavery, and the wrath of God was the first expression of an idea that was beginning to crystallize in Lincoln's mind during the year or two before the presidential election of 1860. He had begun to consider the possibility that God had developed a special plan for the United States, that God was guiding the American republic toward some end. Lincoln did not quite understand God's blueprint for the nation at this point in his life, but he sensed that slavery would, ultimately, not be a part of God's design. Reinhold Niebuhr likens Lincoln to the ancient Hebrew prophets "who first conceived the idea of a meaningful history."[22] For the Hebrew prophets, and for Lincoln, history was not a random series of events; it was no tale told by an idiot full of sound and fury and signifying nothing. It was a sequence of related episodes, each contributing to some predetermined end. Lincoln was coming to believe in a living history, guided and shaped by the Almighty.

By embracing this idea, Lincoln was emulating the Hebrew prophets as well as the American Puritans, who saw themselves as part of God's plan to build a community of God on earth. The covenant that God had struck with the ancient Israelites had been renewed with Puritans of the seventeenth century. Just as the Israelites had escaped captivity in Egypt and journeyed to the promised land of Canaan, the Puritans had escaped from the Old World and settled in Massachusetts. So believed the first Puritan settlers. They had come to the American wilderness to do God's errand, to create the Christian community that God had planned for his newly chosen people. John Winthrop articulated the meaning of the Puritan errand in his influential 1630 sermon, "A Model of Christian Charity," delivered aboard the *Arbella* prior to its landing in Massachusetts. The Puritan settlers would form a community, knit with Christian love, whose goal would be "to improve our lives to do more service to the Lord . . . [so] that ourselves and posterity may be better preserved from the common corruptions of this evil world, to serve the Lord and work out our salvation under the power and purity of his holy ordinances."[23]

Near the end of his sermon, Winthrop defined the meaning of the journey that he and his people were undertaking:

> We shall find that the God of Israel is among us. . . . For we must consider that we shall be as a city upon a hill. The eyes of all people are upon us, so that if we shall deal falsely with our God in this work we have undertaken, and so cause him to withdraw his present help from us, we shall be made a story and a by-word through the world. We shall open the mouths of enemies to speak evil of the ways of God, and all professors of God's sake. We shall shame the faces of many of God's worthy servants, and cause their prayers to be turned into curses upon us till we be consumed out of the good land whither we are going.[24]

The notion of America as a "city upon a hill"—a model community, blessed and guided by God, for the rest of the world to observe and emulate—echoes through American history. The image of the city upon the hill recurs in Puritan rhetoric of the seventeenth and eighteenth centuries. The founders of the American republic appealed to the idea when they declared their independence from Great Britain. God had created human beings with rights, and only a democratic government could protect those rights. Therefore, the American cause was blessed by God. In the late 1850s, Lincoln was appealing to the same spirit. According to Lincoln, God was guiding the American experiment in popular government. Slavery was an affront to the nation's ideals, eloquently articulated in the Declaration of Independence. Lincoln had said, in Peoria in 1854, that he hated slavery because it "deprives our republican example of its just influence in the world"; it "causes the real friends of freedom to doubt our sincerity"

(2:255). Lincoln believed that slavery was taking the nation off the path that God had laid out for it; legal human bondage was a form of despotism, and God would one day call the country into account.

It is not surprising that at this time, the late 1850s, Lincoln began using more biblical language and allusions in his public addresses. Edmund Wilson states that "the Bible was the book he knew best; he had it at his fingertips and quoted it more often than anything else."[25] Lincoln consulted the Bible frequently and could pull a clause from it to suit almost any occasion. His most effective use of the Bible in a speech before the Civil War was the House Divided speech, which kicked off his Senate campaign against Douglas in 1858. In that speech, Lincoln used a line from Matthew 12:25 (or Mark 3:25) to make his argument about how the slavery issue would ultimately be resolved:

> "A house divided against itself cannot stand."
> I believe this government cannot endure, permanently half *slave* and half *free*.
> I do not expect the Union to be *dissolved*—I do not expect the house to *fall*—but I *do* expect it will cease to be divided.
> It will become *all* one thing, or *all* the other. (2:461)

Like a Puritan minister delivering a sermon, Lincoln explicated his biblical text and then provided an application to the present reality. He explained to his audience the dangerous steps that the federal government was taking to nationalize slavery—enacting the Kansas-Nebraska Act and issuing the *Dred Scott* decision. In Lincoln's mind, the divided house became a metaphor for the condition of the United States in the late 1850s.

As his presidency approached and the Union commenced to collapse, Lincoln began to articulate the idea that God would guide the nation through its difficulties and would use Lincoln as his instrument. When he departed Springfield for Washington on February 11, 1861, Lincoln conveyed this point to his friends and supporters:

> To-day I leave you; I go to assume a task more difficult than that which devolved upon General Washington. Unless the great God who assisted

him, shall be with and aid me, I must fail. But if the same omniscient mind, and Almighty arm that directed and protected him, shall guide and support me, I shall not fail, I shall succeed. Let us pray that the God of our fathers may not forsake us now. To him I commend you all—permit me to ask that with equal security and faith, you will invoke His wisdom and guidance for me. (4:191)

As inauguration day approached, Lincoln expressed his hope that the God who guided and protected Washington through the difficult days of the early republic would also steer Lincoln and the nation through the troubles of 1861.

Lincoln hit a similar chord in his address to the New Jersey Senate in Trenton on February 21, 1861, less than two weeks before his inauguration. He began the short speech by recalling the great battles of the Revolutionary War that had taken place in New Jersey, particularly George Washington's crossing of the Delaware River at Trenton to surprise the Hessian troops stationed there on Christmas Day of 1776. Lincoln suggested that the colonists fought for something more than independence; they fought for "something that held out a great promise to all people of the world to all time to come" (4:236). They battled the British to preserve the city upon the hill, the model community that the rest of the world would someday emulate. Then Lincoln invoked God to use himself as an instrument to continue the struggle begun by the American colonists in 1776: "I am exceedingly anxious that this Union, the Constitution, and the liberties of the people shall be perpetuated in accordance with the original idea for which that struggle was made, and I shall be most happy indeed if I shall be an humble instrument in the hands of the Almighty, and of this, his almost chosen people, for perpetuating the object of that great struggle" (4:236). Here Lincoln echoed the Puritan claim that the people of America were chosen by God for a special destiny, that the Americans would play a special role in world affairs. Lincoln insinuated that God had guided Washington and his troops at Trenton in 1776 and that God would also guide Lincoln, who, in turn, would continue the struggle begun by the Americans of Washington's time.

On March 4, 1861, Lincoln delivered his First Inaugural Address to a divided nation. Seven Southern states had already voted to secede from the Union by the time Lincoln took his oath of office. In that address, Lincoln extended his hand in friendship to the South. He pledged not to interfere with slavery where it existed; he announced his belief that the Fugitive Slave Law was backed by the Constitution; he promised not to use force against the states attempting to withdraw from the Union. He made it clear to both the North and the South that the nation can continue half slave and half free, that God would eventually determine a resolution of the slavery issue: "If the Almighty Ruler of nations, with his eternal truth and justice, be on your side of the North, or on yours of the South, that truth, and that justice, will surely prevail, by the judgment of this great tribunal, the American people" (4:270). In other words, God would guide the American people toward a resolution of the great issue that was dividing the nation and threatening the Union.

Near the conclusion of the First Inaugural Address, Lincoln stressed that there was no need for the South to engage in drastic actions: "If it were admitted that you who are dissatisfied, hold the right side in this dispute, there still is no single good reason for precipitate action. Intelligence, patriotism, Christianity, and a firm reliance on Him, who has never yet forsaken this favored land, are still competent to adjust, in the best way, all our present difficulty" (4:271). In this last sentence, Lincoln clearly reiterated his belief that God would ultimately guide the nation—"this favored land"—toward a solution to the serious problem at hand. The resolution of the slavery issue was, in Lincoln's view, part of God's plan for the country.

Alfred Kazin suggests that Lincoln's God "was born of war."[26] Surely Lincoln's faith deepened during the war. Even before the war, however, Lincoln's speeches clearly reveal that the Victorian skeptic, the infidel from Springfield, was already beginning to see the slavery debate and the division between North and South in religious terms. Although he had never joined his parents' church, he had retained the idea from his youth that a judgmental God ruled the universe, a God who punished sinners for their offenses. He had come to believe that slavery was, perhaps, one of the offenses that would one day result in God's severe retribution. He had also embraced the notion, first articulated by the seventeenth-century Puritan settlers of Massachusetts, that the American republic was a special nation, a city upon a hill for the rest of the world to emulate, and that God would offer special guidance to the American people so that their experiment in popular government might continue.

Wolf states that Lincoln's religion was "not static, but dynamic in its development," that Lincoln found his way "to ever deeper levels of faith in response to family suffering and national tragedy."[27] The great national tragedy that would commence shortly after Lincoln delivered his First Inaugural Address would both deepen and test his faith. He would see, even more clearly than before the war, God's hand in the nation's fortunes. He would ask the American people many times to seek God's help in resolving the great conflict that had visited their nation. But the Civil War would also test Lincoln's faith and shake his religious assumptions. He would begin to question why the God who guided his nation, the God who favored this "almost chosen people," would bring upon it and its citizens such a devastating tragedy. If God's plan called for a resolution of the slavery issue, why then did so much blood have to be shed to reach that resolution? By the time of his Second Inaugural Address, Lincoln would have formulated a terrifying response to this question.

FOUR

Lincoln's War, 1861–62:
"I Would Save the Union"

IN HIS FIRST INAUGURAL ADDRESS, Abraham Lincoln extended his hand in friendship to the rebellious Southern states. He closed the address with the words, "We are not enemies, but friends. We must not be enemies" (4:271). Just one month after he spoke these words of healing, however, war broke out between North and South at Fort Sumter, after Lincoln refused South Carolina's demand that the federal fort be evacuated. Even before Lincoln could complete his political appointments for his new administration, the cold war between the North and the South over the secession crisis turned into a hot war of rebellion. Eventually, four more Southern states joined the original seven seceders. Four other slave states—Delaware, Maryland, Kentucky, and Missouri—for the time remained loyal to the Union, but secessionist sentiment ran high in all four; Lincoln would have to work hard to keep them from joining the rebellion.

No free state considered secession—obviously because a Lincoln presidency did not threaten the North in any way. Eleven slave states had withdrawn from the Union because their citizens believed that Lincoln, whom Southerners saw as a Black Republican and an abolitionist, endangered their way of life. From its very beginning, then, the Civil War was, for the South, a conflict over slavery; the Southern states would not have taken the drastic step of withdrawal from the Union if they did not believe that the Lincoln administration posed a serious threat to their peculiar institution. For Lincoln, however, the war between the North and South, when it broke out, was not one over slavery. Slavery could remain where it already existed, Lincoln had asserted many times during the past several years; he had pledged not to interfere with the institution, even though he judged it morally wrong. For Lincoln, the conflict ignited by South Carolina's attack on Fort Sumter, at least initially, concerned the issue of secession and his view of democratic government. But Lincoln's initial outlook on the conflict was subject to change.

In his First Inaugural Address, Lincoln had stated that "the Union of these States is perpetual. Perpetuity is implied, if not expressed, in the fundamental law of all national governments" (4:264). The Constitution, in Lincoln's view, contained no provision for the destruction of the Union. Even if the Constitution were merely a contract signed by the individual states, "can it, as a contract, be peaceably unmade, by less than all the parties who made it?" Lincoln asked. "One party to a contract may violate it—break it, so to speak; but does it not require all to lawfully rescind it?" (4:265). According to Lincoln, the perpetuity of the Union "is confirmed by the history of the Union itself" (4:265). The Union even predates the Constitution; it was formed by the Articles of Association in 1774 and "was matured and continued" by the Declaration of Independence in 1776, the Articles of Confederation of 1778, and the Constitution, whose preamble pledged "a more perfect union" (4:265). Lincoln maintained that no part of the Union could lawfully remove itself, that "*resolves* and *ordinances* to that effect are legally void; and that acts of violence, within any State or States, against the authority of the United States, are insurrectionary or revolutionary, according to circumstances" (4:265). By attacking Fort Sumter, South Carolina had engaged in an act of rebellion. In a message to Congress on July 4, 1861, three months after the start of the war, Lincoln referred to secession as "rebellion thus sugar-coated" (4:433).

The war that was developing at the beginning of his presidency was, for Lincoln, also a test of popular or democratic government. He had campaigned on a platform committed to the position that slavery ought not to be extended, and he had won the election fairly. In Lincoln's view, the South was legally and morally obligated to abide by the results of that election; the rules of democratic government demanded that. In the seventy years since the enactment of the Constitution, the United States had developed the idea of a loyal political opposition. The losing side in an election or any political dispute would have to abide by the fairly resolved result; the losing side would be free to hold and articulate its political positions, to criticize the winners, but the losers would not attempt to destroy the government. Democratic government required loyal losers; it required the minority to submit to the majority's will. According to Don E. Fehrenbacher, this principle was, for Lincoln, "most clearly at stake in the war."[1]

Lincoln did not believe that the existence of slavery in the South caused the rebellion that commenced in April 1861. In his July 4, 1861, address to a special session of Congress, called to deal with the secession crisis and the accompanying war, Lincoln clearly outlined what was, in his view, at stake in the conflict that had begun at Fort Sumter:

> And this issue embraces more than the fate of these United States. It presents to the whole family of man, the question, whether a constitutional republic, or a democracy—a government of the people, by the same people—can, or cannot, maintain its territorial integrity, against its own domestic foes. It presents the question, whether discontented individuals, too few in numbers to control administration, according to organic law, in any case, can always, upon the pretences made in this case, or any other pretences, or arbitrarily, without any pretence, break up their Government, and thus practically put an end to free government upon the earth. (4:426)

Lincoln asserted that the states remaining loyal to the Union must "demonstrate to the world, that those who can fairly carry an election, can also suppress a rebellion"; the North must show "men that what they cannot take by an election, neither can they take it by a war" (4:439).

The long July 4th address to Congress, covering about twenty pages in *The Collected Works of Abraham Lincoln*, did not even mention slavery. Commenting on the address, David Herbert Donald states that Lincoln "put the issue before the country simply as one of Union versus Disunion."[2] Near the end of the speech, Lincoln assured the South, as he had done in his First Inaugural Address, that his administration's goal was a return to the status quo of 1860:

> Lest there be some uneasiness in the minds of candid men, as to what is to be the course of the government, towards the Southern States, *after* the rebellion shall have been suppressed, the Executive deems it proper to say, it will be his purpose then, as ever, to be guided by the Constitution, and the laws; and that he probably will have no different understanding of the powers, and duties of the Federal government, relatively to the rights of the States, and the people, under the Constitution, than that expressed in the inaugural address. (4:439)

In other words, the rebellious South could return to the Union with slavery in place. In July 1861, the war ignited by the attack on Fort Sumter was not, for Lincoln, a war over slavery; South Carolina had incited a rebellion that the federal government was obligated to suppress to preserve the Union and the spirit of popular government.

For Lincoln, the war, in 1861, could not be one over slavery. Four slave states had thus far remained loyal to the Union. One of those states was Maryland; it along with Virginia, which had seceded after the Fort Sumter attack, surrounded Washington, D.C. If Lincoln, in 1861, turned the Southern rebellion into a crusade to abolish slavery, Maryland and the other border slave states—Missouri, Kentucky, Delaware—might also vote to withdraw from the Union. Maryland's secession would probably necessitate abandoning the capital, moving it to safer ground in the North. Such a move would provide the South with an important moral and political victory and might convince foreign nations to recognize the South as an independent country, an action that Great Britain and other foreign powers were considering. Lincoln was also unsure whether the North would support a war over slavery. Would the Northern states provide thousands of men to fight a war whose aim was to abolish slavery? Furthermore, Lincoln, as James McPherson points out, doubted whether he had the constitutional power to wage a war against slavery; he had, on March 4, 1861, taken an oath to protect the Constitution, and the Constitution protected slavery.[3]

Through the first sixteen months of the war, Lincoln stood firmly by the statements that he had made about slavery during the presidential campaign and in his First Inaugural Address, despite pressure from abolitionists to turn the conflict into a crusade to uproot slavery. Republicans like Senator Charles Sumner of Massachusetts and Senator Benjamin Wade of Ohio were prompting Lincoln to make the abolition of slavery a war aim. Abolitionist crusaders such as Frederick Douglass, Henry Ward Beecher, and William Lloyd Garrison were advancing the same argument. Other Union politicians were demanding that the South be punished for its act of insurrection and that the punishment ought to be in the form of a general emancipation. But Lincoln steadfastly refused to consider emancipating the slaves or making emancipation a goal of the war. In fact, Lincoln took decisive steps to separate the secession issue and the slavery issue. In August 1861, when General John Frémont effected an order to free the slaves of Confederate supporters in Missouri, Lincoln immediately rebuked the general, stating that liberating slaves "will alarm our Southern Union friends, and turn them against us—perhaps ruin our rather fair prospect for Kentucky" (4:506). Lincoln asked Frémont to modify his order to comply with a bill passed by Congress earlier in August that allowed federal armies to confiscate the property of Southerners used *directly* in the war effort. Lerone Bennett Jr. is correct when he states that Lincoln's initial policy was "to win the war without touching slavery."[4]

But Lincoln was wise enough to realize that terminating the Southern rebellion only to return the country to the unstable condition of 1860 would be senseless. Another crisis would surely produce a second effort at secession. Something had to be done about the major issue dividing North and South. Abolition was not an option for Lincoln in 1861; the South would not rejoin a Union in which slavery was prohibited, and Lincoln did not believe that he could persuade the North to accept abolition as a war aim. Lincoln's solution was a plan for gradual, compensated emancipation. Individual states, not the federal government, would set time periods for the freeing of their slaves, and the federal government, in turn, would compensate the states for their acts of emancipation so that the state governments could then compensate individual slaveholders. In November 1861, Lincoln helped draft an emancipation bill for Delaware that would pay the state, in 6 percent federal bonds, $719,200 if the state freed all of its slaves by some future date. (One version of the bill mandated emancipation by 1867, another by 1893.) To Lincoln's disappointment, the bill was never introduced in the Delaware legislature.

Lincoln's failure in Delaware, however, did not dissuade him from continuing to advance the policy of gradual, compensated emancipation. On March 6, 1862, a year into his presidency, Lincoln, in a message to Congress, recommended the adoption of such a policy. Lincoln argued that the implementation of a plan for gradual, compensated emancipation by the four loyal slave states would end the rebellious states' hopes that the loyal four would join the rebellion. He stated that "gradual, and not sudden emancipation, is better for all" (5:145). He also pointed out that compensated emancipation would be, in the long term, cheaper than financing the war. Eight days later, Lincoln, using an accountant's ledger, showed, in a letter to Senator James McDougall of California, that "less than one half-day's cost of this war would pay for all the slaves in Delaware at four hundred dollars per head" and that "less than eighty-seven days cost of this war would, at the same price, pay for all [slaves] in Delaware, Maryland, District of Columbia, Kentucky, and Missouri" (5:160). Lincoln assured McDougall that "taking the initiatory steps on the part of those states and this District, would shorten the war more than eighty-seven days" (5:160).

Lincoln pressed for gradual, compensated emancipation through the spring and early summer of 1862. On July 12, 1862, he gathered twenty-eight representatives from the four loyal border states to the White House to urge them to promote, in their home states, his plan for gradual, compensated emancipation. Lincoln reiterated his belief that adopting such an emancipation plan would send a clear signal to the rebellious states that the loyal four intended to remain within the Union. He advised them to accept payment for slaves now, in exchange for gradual emancipation, "lest the war ere long render us pecuniarily unable to do so" (5:318). He reminded the representatives of these four states that the colonization of freed slaves was still an option: "Room in South America for colonization, can be obtained cheaply, and in abundance; and when numbers shall be large enough to be company and encouragement for one another, the freed people will not be so reluctant to go" (5:318). Lincoln also informed them that pressure was mounting for general emancipation, and he suggested that their acceptance of his plan for gradual emancipation might ease the pressure for freeing all slaves everywhere in the Union.

Two days later, Lincoln sent to Congress another bill for gradual, compensated emancipation. That same day, however, he received a reply signed by twenty of the twenty-eight border state representatives who had attended the White House meeting of July 12. They rejected his emancipation plan. But Lincoln still remained hopeful, through the end of 1862, that his plan for gradual, compensated emancipation might be the ultimate solution for the slavery issue in the United States. If he could garner political support for such a policy, slavery could, over three or four decades, be eliminated from American soil, and individuals affected would be fairly compensated.

In reality, Lincoln's plan for gradual emancipation was a long shot. Certainly the rebellious slaves states would have no part of it. In the summer of 1862, they were winning the war, or at least they were steadfastly prohibiting the North from forcing them back into the Union. They had decisively stopped the North's first serious offensive, at Bull Run in July 1861. They had foiled General George McClellan's Peninsular Campaign during the spring and early summer of 1862. General Ulysses S. Grant had won important victories in the war's western theater, but a Confederate army had dealt him a heavy blow, if not a defeat, in Tennessee at Shiloh in April 1862. (At the end of August, Confederate armies would win another major victory at Bull Run.) Above all, the South had convinced Lincoln and the North that forcing the rebellious states back into the Union would entail fighting a long and bloody war, a conflict from which Northerners might eventually withdraw support.

The four loyal border states also showed little interest in Lincoln's plan for gradual, compensated emancipation. The slaveholding loyalists, too, wanted slavery to remain intact within their borders, and they knew that Lincoln lacked the ability to force emancipation upon them. If he attempted to interfere with slavery, the border states could simply join the Confederacy—an action that Lincoln was determined to prevent at all costs. The loyalists assumed, incorrectly perhaps, that the rebellious states would eventually be forced backed into the Union with slavery in place; perhaps the price that the North would have to pay to reunite the nation would be to allow the passage of a constitutional amendment protecting slavery where it already existed forever into the future. (Such a compromise had already been discussed in the early months of the secession crisis.) With that prospect on the horizon, the loyal slave states saw no merit in accepting Lincoln's plan for gradual, compensated emancipation; they never considered it seriously.

According to LaWanda Cox, Lincoln advocated a gradual, compensated emancipation because he "sought the largest possible degree of legal security and popular acceptance for an initial move against slavery."[5] But Lincoln was certainly shrewd enough to see that his careful initial effort against slavery had few backers, so he explored other options. Where it was legally possible to do so, he moved boldly against slavery. In April 1862, he signed a bill passed by Congress outlawing slavery in Washington, D.C. Since the Constitution gave Congress jurisdiction over Washington, Lincoln felt legally correct in acting against slavery there. "I have never doubted the constitutional authority of congress to abolish slavery in this District," he wrote in his message to Congress of April 16, 1862, "and I have ever desired to see the national capital freed from the institution in some satisfactory way" (5:192).

A month later, Lincoln subtly revealed that he was also considering a more assertive move against slavery than gradual, compensated emancipation. Ironically, Lincoln signaled his new tactic in a proclamation in which he again rebuked a general in the federal army for attempting to liberate the slaves in the areas under his jurisdiction. On May 9, 1862, General David Hunter, headquartered in Hilton Head, South Carolina, and in charge of a division called the Department of the South, issued General Order Number 11, which established martial law in South Carolina, Georgia, and Florida. General Hunter's order also declared that "slavery and martial law in a free country are altogether incompatible; the persons in these three

States—Georgia, Florida and South Carolina—heretofore held as slaves, are therefore declared forever free" (5:222).

Lincoln quickly revoked Hunter's order, as he had done to General Frémont's order the year before:

> I, Abraham Lincoln, President of the United States, proclaim and declare, that the government of the United States, had no knowledge, information, or belief, of an intention on the part of General Hunter to issue such a proclamation. . . . And further, that neither General Hunter, nor any other commander, or person, has been authorized by the Government of the United States to make proclamations declaring the slaves of any State free; and that the supposed proclamation, now in question, whether genuine or false, is altogether void, so far as respects such declaration. (5:222)

But Lincoln added a point to his proclamation of nullification that, according to Mark E. Neely Jr., signaled a change in Lincoln's thinking concerning the power to emancipate American slaves:

> I further make known that whether it be competent for me, as Commander-in-Chief of the Army and Navy, to declare the Slaves of any state or states, free, and whether at any time, in any case, it shall have become a necessity indispensable to the maintenance of the government, to exercise such supposed power, are questions which, under my responsibility, I reserve to myself, and which I can not feel justified in leaving to the decision of commanders in the field. (5:222–23)

Neely suggests that Lincoln was claiming, for the first time, the right to free the slaves as an act of military necessity. He had previously maintained that only the states held the right to emancipate slaves within their borders.[6] Lincoln ended his proclamation by reiterating his support for gradual, compensated emancipation, but he had clearly, in the same proclamation, hinted that he was weighing other options for freeing the slaves.

A few months later, Lincoln penned the often-quoted letter to Horace Greeley, editor of the *New York Tribune*. The *Tribune*, on August 20, 1862, had printed a letter by Greeley to Lincoln, under the title "The Prayer of Twenty Millions," that criticized Lincoln for trying to conduct the war while ignoring the slavery issue. Greeley asserted, among other accusations, that Lincoln was "unduly influenced by the counsels . . . of certain fossil politicians hailing from the Border Slave States" (5:389). On August 22, Lincoln responded to Greeley's letter so as not to "leave any one in doubt" (5:388) about his policy on the emancipation of the slaves:

> I would save the Union. I would save it the shortest way under the Constitution. . . . My paramount object in this struggle *is* to save the Union, and is *not* either to save or destroy slavery. If I could save the Union without freeing *any* slave I would do it, and if I could save it by freeing *all* the slaves I would do it; and if I could save it by freeing some and leaving others alone I would also do that. What I do about slavery, and the colored race, I do because I believe it helps to save the Union; and what I forbear, I forbear because I do *not* believe it would help to save the Union. I shall do *less* whenever I shall believe what I am doing hurts the cause, and I shall do *more* whenever I shall believe doing more will help the cause. (5:388–89)

Lincoln concluded the letter by contrasting his personal belief and his professional duty regarding the issue of slavery: "I have here stated my purpose according to my view of *official* duty; and I intend no modification of my oft-expressed *personal* wish that all men every where could be free" (5:389).

In this letter to Greeley, Lincoln was reemphasizing the point that the war primarily concerned the Union, not the institution of slavery—a position he had held consistently since the Confederate guns blasted away at Fort Sumter. Nonetheless, he was also signaling, in a public forum, that he would be willing to free the slaves if it advanced his primary goal of preserving the Union. Donald states that the letter to Greeley proves that, in Lincoln's mind, "there was no necessary disjunction between a war for the Union and a war to end slavery."[7] Fehrenbacher argues that Lincoln's letter to Greeley was "not a statement of policy but instead a brilliant piece of propaganda," that Lincoln was preparing the public for the controversial step of complete emancipation by "adhering scrupulously to the fiction that this momentous step was strictly a military measure."[8]

Fehrenbacher might be correct. A month earlier, Lincoln had already decided that a general emancipation might be necessary to win the war and thereby save the Union. On July 22, 1862, a month before he sent the letter to Greeley, Lincoln had shared with the members of his cabinet the draft of a document urging the rebellious Southern states "to cease participating in . . . the existing rebellion . . . and to return to their proper allegiance to the United States, on pain of the forfeitures and seizures" of property, which included slaves (5:336). But Lincoln was certainly viewing emancipation strictly as a war measure. If the South were to heed his order and return to the Union, slavery would remain in place. Lincoln was not intending to strike against slavery for moral reasons, though he personally believed, as stated in the letter to Greeley, that "all men every where" should be free. Lincoln, in the summer of 1862, was advancing emancipation as a means of curtailing the conflict that was rending the Union or at least making certain that the conflict, if it were to continue, would ultimately achieve some finality on the slavery issue. By this time, Lincoln was wise enough to realize that winning the war and forcing the South back into the Union would be almost pointless if slavery were to remain legal; the South would surely secede again as soon as some new crisis developed over slavery. Lincoln had no takers for his plan for gradual, compensated emancipation. He had to chart another course. Richard Hofstadter might be correct when he states, "When Lincoln at last determined, in July 1862, to move toward emancipation, it was only after all his other policies had failed."[9]

But Lincoln was less than completely confident in this new course of action; he was still grappling with the contradiction between his personal preference that "all men every where" be free and his official duty as president to protect the Constitution and to respect the rights of the individual states. His mind, indeed, remained a divided house through the summer of 1862. Lincoln's ambivalence is clearly evident in his reply of September 13, 1862, to a memorial in favor of general emancipation presented by a congregation of Chicago Christians. Lincoln conceded, in his reply, that slavery was the cause of the war: "I admit that slavery is the root of the rebellion, or at least its *sine qua non*. The ambition of politicians may have instigated them to the act, but they would have been impotent without slavery as their instrument" (5:423). Yet he frankly admitted that general emancipation, while the war continued, might neither end the rebellion nor free any slaves: "What *good* would a proclamation of emancipation from me do, especially as we are now situated? I do not want to issue a document that the world over will see must necessarily be inoperative, like the Pope's bull against the comet! Would *my word* free the slaves, when I cannot even enforce the Constitution in the rebel States?" (5:420). He resolved to continue to consider emancipation only as a war measure to be employed by the commander in chief of the armed forces:

> Now, then, tell me, if you please, what possible result of good would follow the issuing of such a proclamation as you desire? Understand, I raise no objections against it on legal or constitutional grounds; for, as commander-in-chief of the army and navy, in time of war, I suppose I have a right to take any measure which may best subdue the enemy. . . . I view the matter as a practical war measure, to be decided upon according to the advantages or disadvantages it may offer to the suppression of the rebellion. (5:421)

Lincoln made these statements four days before the Battle of Antietam. Five days after the battle, he would issue a Preliminary Emancipation Proclamation.

The war was prompting Lincoln to bend on the issue of slavery, but it was not affecting his attitudes on race. Through the first twenty months of the war, Lincoln continued to push for a colonization plan that would result in the United States becoming a whites-only nation. In his annual message to Congress of December 3, 1861, Lincoln promoted colonization for all slaves freed through the war or by any plan for compensated emancipation, "in a climate congenial to them" (5:48). Lincoln added, "It might be well to consider, too,—whether the free colored people already in the United States could not, so far as individuals may desire, be included in such colonization" (5:48). He would continue to push for colonization until he issued the Emancipation Proclamation on January 1, 1863.

Further evidence that Lincoln's attitudes on race remained unshaken during the first twenty months of the war appears in his policy and comments on the use of African American troops. Since the start of the conflict, Frederick Douglass and other abolitionist leaders were strongly urging Lincoln to arm African Americans. When Lincoln, the day after the fall of Fort Sumter, called for seventy-five thousand volunteers to put down the rebellion, African Americans quickly responded and formed militia units in Pittsburgh, Philadelphia, and Providence, Rhode Island, but the Department of War decided not to enlist African American soldiers. Several weeks after the North's disastrous defeat in the First Battle of Bull Run, Douglass wrote an editorial titled "Fighting the Rebels with Only One Hand" in his abolitionist newspaper, *Douglass' Monthly*, in which he sharply criticized Lincoln and the War Department's policy:

> Our Presidents, Governors, Generals and Secretaries are calling, with almost frantic vehemence for men.—"Men! Men! Send us men!" they scream, or the cause of the Union is gone . . . and yet these very officers, representing the people and the Government, steadily and persistently refuse to receive the very class of men which have a deeper interest in the defeat and humiliation of the rebels, than all others. . . . What a spectacle of blind, unreasoning prejudice and pusillanimity is this! The national edifice is on fire. Every man who can carry a bucket of water, or remove a brick, is wanted; but those who have the care of the building . . . are determined that the flames shall only be extinguished by Indo-Caucasian hands, and to have the building burnt rather than save it by means of any other. Such is the pride, the stupid prejudice and folly that rules the hour.[10]

But Douglass's stinging editorial—and others like it—did not immediately prompt Lincoln and his War Department to change their policy regarding African American soldiers. The Union army would remain, at least during the first year of the war, a whites-only institution.

As the war entered its second year, however, Lincoln realized that it would not soon end and that he would need scores of thousands of men to fight it. In July 1862, Congress initiated the recruitment of African American troops under the Confiscation Act. Lincoln responded by stating that he had no objection to recruiting free blacks, the slaves of disloyal owners, or the slaves of loyal owners with the owners' consent (5:338). Nonetheless, no official recruitment of African American soldiers took place in 1862. General Hunter assembled a regiment of African American troops in South Carolina during the summer of 1862, but the War Department refused to authorize the unit, and it essentially disbanded. At the same time, in Kansas, General James H. Lane recruited two companies of former slaves and African American freemen, but the War Department also refused recognition of those companies. In Louisiana, General Benjamin Butler raised three regiments of African American soldiers and, in November 1862, placed them in the field, even though the War Department did not officially muster them into service until the following year.

On August 4, 1862, two members of Congress and an accompanying delegation met with Lincoln at the White House to offer two African American regiments from Indiana. Lincoln explained that he "was not prepared to go the length of enlisting negroes as soldiers." He suggested that enlisting black soldiers might result in Kentucky's secession from the Union, that "to arm the negroes would turn 50,000 bayonets from the loyal Border States against us that were for us" (5:357). The following month, Lincoln offered another explanation why he had instructed the War Department not to recruit African American regiments. His audience this time was the delegation of Chicago Christians who were strongly urging a general emancipation. He conceded that emancipating the slaves might weaken the South by "drawing off their laborers," but he wondered what would be done with the ex-slaves: "But I am not sure we could do much with the blacks. If we were to arm them, I fear that in a few weeks the arms would be in the hands of the rebels" (5:423).

Lincoln's comment to this Chicago delegation reveals that his opposition to the use of African American troops was not merely political—a concern that the loyal slave states might object. He also had serious doubts about the performance of black soldiers in combat; he reasoned that their weapons would soon be in the hands of the enemy, though he did not elaborate why or how that would happen. Did Lincoln actually believe that black soldiers raised in the South might betray the Union cause and join forces with the Confederates? Or would black soldiers prove to be cowards under fire and drop their weapons and flee the battlefield? Would blacks be impossible to train for combat and be easily forced to surrender? Lincoln revealed in this address to the Chicago Christian delegation that he had embraced the prejudices and stereotypes held by many white Americans—that blacks were ignorant and untrainable and that they lacked the courage and discipline to become good soldiers.

Ten days after he addressed the Chicago Christians, Lincoln summoned a group of distinguished African Americans from Washington, D.C., to the White House and revealed, in one of the most startling addresses of his political career, that on issues of race, he had not changed very much, that he still held the attitudes articulated in the debates with Stephen Douglas during the Senate campaign of 1858. Lincoln's opening remarks concerned colonization:

> Why should they [African Americans] leave this country? This is, perhaps, the first question for proper consideration. You and we are different races. We have between us a broader difference than exists between almost any other two races. Whether it is right or wrong I need not discuss, but this physical difference is a great disadvantage to us both, as I think your race suffer very greatly, many of them by living among us, while ours suffer from your presence. In a word we suffer on each side. If this is admitted, it affords a reason at least why we should be separated. (5:371)

Lincoln conceded that African Americans "are suffering . . . the greatest wrong inflicted on any people" and that "even when you cease to be slaves, you are yet far removed from being placed on an equality with the white race" (5:371–72). He condemned slavery and "its evil effects on the white race" (5:372). Then, in a startlingly harsh statement, Lincoln blamed the war on African Americans, not on the rebellious South and its slaveholders:

> See our present condition—the country engaged in war!—our white men cutting one another's throats, none knowing how far it will extend; and then consider what we know to be the truth. But for your race among us there could not be war, although many men engaged on either side do not care for you one way or the other. Nevertheless, I repeat, without

the institution of Slavery and the colored race as its basis, the war could not have an existence. (5:372)

Lincoln, as he had done before becoming president, again made the case in this address for separating the races by moving African Americans to another continent. He allowed that many African Americans believed that they could live more comfortably in the United States than in a foreign country, but he considered this "an extremely selfish view of the case" (5:372). He suggested that many slave owners might free their slaves if they knew that the slaves would leave America. Lincoln encouraged his audience to "sacrifice something of your present comfort for the purpose of being as grand in that as the white people" (5:373). He called on black Americans to imitate George Washington, who "endured greater physical hardships than if he had remained a British subject. Yet he was a happy man, because he was engaged in benefiting his race" (5:373).

Lincoln did not advocate emigration to Liberia; he realized that Africa might be too far for many African Americans to travel. Instead, Lincoln suggested emigration to Central America. He spoke of a region rich in coal, which "will afford an opportunity to the inhabitants for immediate employment till they get ready to settle permanently in their homes" (5:374). Referring to the coal mines, Lincoln said, "I think I see the means available for your self-reliance" (5:374). Lincoln concluded his address with a feeble plea for volunteers for his Central American colonization plan: "Could I get a hundred tolerably intelligent men, with their wives and children, to 'cut their own fodder,' so to speak? Can I have fifty? If I could find twenty-five able-bodied men, with a mixture of women and children . . . I think I could make a successful commencement" (5:375).[11]

Upon hearing of this address, Frederick Douglass, who was not present for it, lashed out against Lincoln in *Douglass' Monthly*. Douglass said that Lincoln sounded like "an itinerant Colonization lecturer," that the president was "showing all his inconsistencies, his pride of race and blood, his contempt for Negroes and his canting hypocrisy." Douglass wondered how "an honest man could creep into such a character as that implied by this address."[12] Douglass, like many other civil rights leaders, believed that the future of African Americans was in a slave-free Union, not in another land.

According to Fehrenbacher, Lincoln's rhetoric of colonization in late 1862 was part of a careful plan to condition white Americans for general emancipation, "a means of quieting fears about the racial consequences of manumission." In Fehrenbacher's view, white Americans would be more receptive to emancipation if they knew that the freed slaves would ultimately end up living on another continent.[13] Similarly, Phillip Shaw Paludan considers Lincoln's address to prominent Washington African American citizens as evidence of his "understanding of racial fears about emancipation. . . . [H]e understood the extent of prejudice in the North and was seeking in colonization some response to it."[14] Neely sees Lincoln's address to Washington's prominent African American citizens, his address to the Chicago Christian delegation, and his letter to Horace Greeley as part of a grand scheme of deception, that Lincoln "chose, without actually lying, to give the American public the impression that he was not likely to free the slaves."[15]

These three Lincoln scholars offer plausible political explanations for Lincoln's persistent push for colonization, which was, of course, a completely unworkable solution to the problems posed by slavery and emancipation and hardly desirable in the eyes of African Americans, unless they found a career in the coal mines attractive. A simpler explanation for Lincoln's continuing advocacy of colonization might be that Lincoln, eighteen months into the war, remained a white supremacist and segregationist; he was not waging a war of racial liberation. Before becoming president, Lincoln had advanced his belief in the superiority of the white race; he had clearly stated his position that African Americans do not deserve to be his political or social equals. Now, eighteen months into his presidency, he judged African Americans unfit for military duty, a basic responsibility of citizenship and a gateway to suffrage and other rights of citizenship. He had been reluctant to free the slaves; now that he was becoming resigned to emancipation as a war measure, he was wary of its result, so he continued to promote colonization—a measure designed to rid America of free African Americans and remake the nation as a whites-only society. Moreover,

Lincoln, in late 1862, was clearly frustrated by the war. Casualties were mounting, and he saw no clear road to a Northern victory. He looked for scapegoats and found them in the slaves. They were the cause of the war. If they only could be banished to some faraway place, the divided nation could return to normal. Then his political party could reintroduce the Whig probusiness agenda of the 1840s.

The Preliminary Emancipation Proclamation, issued on September 22, 1862, merely reiterated Lincoln's hopes for gradual, compensated emancipation followed by a plan for colonization. Neely refers to the document's prose as "leaden legalese."[16] Lincoln first restated his primary war aim—"that hereafter, as heretofore, the war will be prosecuted for the object of practically restoring the constitutional relation between the United States, and each of the states" (5:433–34)—then offered "pecuniary aid" to all states that adopt "immediate, or gradual abolishment of slavery within their respective limits" and continued support "for the effort to colonize persons of African descent, with their consent, upon this continent, or elsewhere, with the previously obtained consent of the Governments existing there" (5:434). Next, Lincoln threatened a limited emancipation—that as of January 1, 1863, slaves held in states still in rebellion against the United States "shall be then, thenceforward, and forever free" (5:434). The remaining pages of the proclamation restated laws already passed by Congress regarding fugitive slaves and the confiscation of property owned by citizens supporting the rebellion.

The Preliminary Emancipation Proclamation was a final plea for gradual, compensated emancipation. If the rebellious Southern states bit on Lincoln's offer, they could return to the Union as slave states, though he strongly urged that they adopt a plan of gradual emancipation. The only change in Lincoln's policy on slavery concerned the January 1, 1863, deadline. If the states in rebellion did not return to the Union by that date, Lincoln would exercise the power that he had claimed in his address to the Chicago Christians: He would issue a general emancipation. Lincoln was moving slowly, perhaps reluctantly, to abolish slavery on American soil.

Lincoln held fast to the policy outlined in the Preliminary Emancipation Proclamation through the end of 1862. On December 1, he made his annual address to Congress. The address, the ancestor of to-day's State of the Union speech, covered a variety of topics, including foreign affairs, the project to extend the telegraph to the West Coast, the nation's financial condition, and relations with American Indian tribes. Benjamin Quarles has pointed out, however, that 40 percent of Lincoln's 9,167 words in that speech referred to compensated emancipation and colonization; these options were definitely still on the table, at the end of 1862, for any slave state, loyal or disloyal, to choose.[17] In this speech, Lincoln even proposed three amendments to the United States Constitution—one to guarantee compensation to any state that freed its slaves by 1900, one to guarantee that any slaves freed during the war would remain forever free, and one to appropriate money for colonization.

Although this address to Congress simply restated Lincoln's support for gradual, compensated emancipation and colonization, it suggested subtle changes in his thinking about the war and the future of freed slaves. In his address to Congress on July 4, 1861, Lincoln had clearly stated that the war that had just begun concerned saving the Union and protecting popular government. That long address had not mentioned slavery. Here, almost eighteen months later, Lincoln identified slavery as the cause of the war: "Without slavery the rebellion could never have existed; without slavery it could not continue" (5:530). At the close of 1862, Lincoln was also giving more thought to what might happen to the nation when the slaves were freed. "I cannot make it better known than it already is, that I strongly favor colonization," Lincoln stated on December 1, 1862. "And yet I wish to say there is an objection urged against free colored persons remaining in the country, which is largely imaginary, if not sometimes malicious" (5:534). Lincoln argued that the freeing of slaves would not reduce the wages of white workers and then, for the first time, presented the possibility of a harmoniously integrated society:

> But is it dreaded that the freed people will swarm forth, and cover the whole land? Are they not already in the land? Will liberation make them any more numerous? Equally distributed among the whites of the whole country, and there would be but one colored to seven whites. Could the

one, in any way, greatly disturb the seven? There are many communities now, having more than one free colored person, to seven whites; and this without any apparent consciousness of evil from it. . . . The District [of Columbia] has more than one free colored to six whites; and yet, in its frequent petitions to Congress, I believe it has never presented the presence of free colored persons as one of its grievances. (5:535)

Lincoln still favored the colonization of free African Americans in another continent, but he was at least preparing the nation for the failure of that policy by suggesting that an integrated American society need not lead to disaster.

Lincoln made it clear, at the end of his address to Congress on December 1, 1862, that he was not backtracking on his commitment to general emancipation that he had announced in September. His proposal for three new constitutional amendments to deal with slavery and freed slaves did not replace the general emancipation that would take effect on January 1, 1863: "Nor will the war, nor proceedings under the proclamation of September 22, 1862, be stayed because of the *recommendation* of this plan" (5:536). Lincoln had taken a long time to decide on general emancipation. Responding to a serenade two days after he issued the Preliminary Emancipation Proclamation, Lincoln told the assembled crowd of citizens, "What I did, I did after very full deliberation, and under a very heavy and solemn sense of responsibility. I can only trust in God I have made no mistake" (5:438). Lincoln was not turning back on that commitment.

Lincoln scholars have debated why he finally arrived at the decision to free the slaves. Some argue that pressure from the abolitionists in the Republican Party finally moved Lincoln toward emancipation. Others argue that pressure from Great Britain motivated Lincoln to act. Since the beginning of the war, a naval blockade of Southern ports had severely limited the exportation of Southern cotton across the Atlantic Ocean. England needed the South's cotton for its textile mills and was considering recognizing the Confederacy, which would also provide the British with an excuse for attempting to break the North's blockade. But the British were vehemently antislavery; they would not join forces with a slave nation in a war being fought to end slavery.

By issuing the Preliminary Emancipation Proclamation, Lincoln was signaling the British that American slavery would be a casualty of his nation's civil war. But perhaps Lincoln finally acted to abolish slavery out of simple desperation. The war was going poorly for the North. With no end to the conflict in sight, Lincoln might have believed that the time had come for some bold and dramatic stroke that would raise the stakes of the struggle.

Some biographers suggest that Lincoln finally decided to issue the Preliminary Emancipation Proclamation on September 22, 1862, because of a deal that he struck with God. Lincoln reportedly told the members of his cabinet on that day that he had made a solemn vow to God that he would free the slaves if God allowed General George McClellan to check General Robert E. Lee's late-summer invasion of the North. Lee had marched his Army of Northern Virginia into Maryland with the intention of moving further northward into Pennsylvania; Lee wished to bring the war to Northern soil and perhaps to capture a key Pennsylvania city. On September 17, 1862, in the bloodiest single day of fighting of the Civil War, McClellan stopped Lee at Antietam Creek near Sharpsburg, Maryland. Lincoln, in turn, decided to announce his Preliminary Emancipation Proclamation.[18]

This story rings true because Lincoln's religious faith deepened during his presidency, perhaps as a result of the overwhelming national tragedy that commenced when Lincoln took office. As Richard N. Current suggests, Lincoln "grew in faith after going to Washington in 1861."[19] This growth manifested itself in several ways. Lincoln, in his speeches, more often called upon God to steer the nation through its present crisis. He concluded his July 4, 1861, address to Congress by asking his audience to "renew our trust in God" (4:441). Lincoln ended a short speech to Evangelical Lutherans on May 13, 1862, by placing the nation's fortunes in the war in God's hands:

> You all may recollect that in taking up the sword thus forced into our hands this Government appealed to the prayers of the pious and the good, and declared that it placed its whole dependence upon the favor of God. I now humbly and reverently, in your presence, reiterate the acknowledgment of that dependence, not doubting that, if it shall please the Divine Being who determines the destinies of nations that this shall

remain a united people, they will, humbly seeking the Divine guidance, make their prolonged national existence a source of new benefits to themselves and their successors, and to all classes and conditions of mankind. (5:212–13)

On August 12, 1861, Lincoln proclaimed the first of several days of public prayer and fasting to secure God's blessings upon the nation. He urged citizens to "acknowledge and revere the Supreme Government of God; to bow in humble submission to his chastisements; to confess and deplore their sins and transgressions . . . and to pray for the pardon of their past offences, and for a blessing upon their present and prospective action" (4:482). Then, sounding like a Puritan preacher, Lincoln identified the current national crisis as God's punishment upon the nation for its sins—a vengeance that he had predicted in his prewar speeches against slavery:

> And whereas, when our own beloved Country, once, by the blessing of God, united, prosperous and happy, is now afflicted with faction and civil war, it is peculiarly fit for us to recognize the hand of God in this terrible visitation, and in sorrowful remembrance of our own faults and crimes as a nation and as individuals, to humble ourselves before Him, and to pray for His mercy,—to pray that we may be spared further punishment, though most justly deserved; that our arms may be blessed and made effectual for the re-establishment of law, order and peace, throughout the wide extent of our country; and that the inestimable boon of civil and religious liberty, earned under His guidance and blessing, by the labors and sufferings of our fathers, may be restored in all its original excellence:— (4:482)

Lincoln was beginning to see the hand of God in the great civil war that had enveloped his country. The following year, on April 10, 1862, Lincoln issued a proclamation of thanksgiving for recent battlefield victories. He urged Americans to assemble in their houses of worship to offer thanks for those victories and to "invoke the Divine Guidance for our national counsels, to the end that they may speedily result in the restoration of peace, harmony, and unity through our borders, and hasten the establishment of fraternal relations among all the countries of the earth" (5:186).

As the war progressed, Lincoln more often expressed his belief that he was an instrument in God's hands, an idea that he had also articulated before assuming the presidency. He told a delegation of Friends who visited the White House on June 20, 1862, that he sometimes felt like "an instrument in God's hands of accomplishing a great work" (5:279). Lincoln elaborated on that idea in his address to the Chicago Christians on September 13, 1862. These visitors to the White House had apparently suggested that God willed the emancipation of the slaves, but Lincoln was not so sure of that: "I hope it will not be irreverent for me to say that if it is probable that God would reveal his will to others, on a point so connected with my duty, it might be supposed he would reveal it directly to me; for, unless I am more deceived in myself than I often am, it is my earnest desire to know the will of Providence in this matter. *And if I can learn what it is I will do it!*" (5:420). Lincoln clearly believed that God would use him as an instrument, but he was not yet certain what specific action God wanted him to take.

Lincoln's faith deepened as the war progressed. Ironically, however, the more Lincoln saw the hand of God in the conflict, the less certain he became of God's will. One of Lincoln's most personally revealing statements, a private Meditation on the Divine Will, written on September 2, 1862, reveals Lincoln's inability to determine with any certitude God's will in the present civil war:

> The will of God prevails. In great contests each party claims to act in accordance with the will of God. Both *may* be, and one *must* be wrong. God can not be *for*, and *against* the same thing at the same time. In the present civil war it is quite possible that God's purpose is something different from the purpose of either party—and yet the human instrumentalities, working just as they do, are of the best adaptation to effect His purpose. I am almost ready to say this is probably true—that God wills this contest, and wills that it shall not end yet. By his mere quiet power, on the minds of the now contestants, He could have either *saved* or *destroyed* the Union without a human contest. Yet the contest began. And having begun He could give the final victory to either side any day. Yet the contest proceeds. (5:403–4)

As Edmund Wilson suggests, Lincoln, as the war continued undecided, "becomes a good deal less sure that the moral issue is perfectly clear, that the Almighty Ruler of nations is committed to the side of the North."[20] Elton Trueblood calls Lincoln's meditation "one of the best exhibitions of the theology of anguish."[21] Allen C. Guelzo states that Lincoln's meditation "contains the most radically metaphysical question ever posed by an American president. Lincoln had come, by the circle of a lifetime and the disasters of the war, to confront once again the Calvinist God . . . who possessed a conscious will to intervene, challenge, and reshape human destinies," the "voice out of the whirlwind speaking to the American Job."[22]

Before the war, Lincoln had seemed certain that God was guiding the American experiment in popular government. Why, then, did God allow this war for disunion to continue? Lincoln wrote his Meditation on the Divine Will the day after a devastating Union defeat at Bull Run. Why had God not given the North a swift victory to ensure the continuance of democratic government? Lincoln had also come to see slavery as a grievous offense that would one day merit God's retribution. Why was God allowing the slaveholding South to inflict such devastating defeats upon the antislavery North? Was the war God's punishment for national sins, as Lincoln suggested in his national fast day proclamation of August 12, 1861? According to William Wolf, Lincoln would not provide "a full and clear answer" to these kinds of questions until he delivered his Second Inaugural Address.[23]

Several weeks after expressing these thoughts in a private meditation, Lincoln revealed them in a letter to Eliza P. Gurney, a Quaker woman who had visited him at the White House. Lincoln explained to Gurney that he was "a humble instrument in the hands of our Heavenly Father" and that he "desired that all my works and acts may be according to his will." But Lincoln confessed that his efforts often failed because God "wills it otherwise." Lincoln admitted that he wished that the war had never commenced or that it had already ended, but "we find that it still continues." God has allowed the war to continue "for some wise purpose of his own, mysterious and unknown to us" (5:478). Lincoln would spend the next two years trying to determine God's mysterious purpose.

As the year 1862 came to a close, Lincoln prepared to issue the Emancipation Proclamation. Perhaps God had willed the document by giving General McClellan the victory over General Lee at Sharpsburg. Perhaps Lincoln himself had willed it. He had always believed slavery to be immoral, but he had been reticent to interfere with it in the places where it already existed. But twenty awful months of war had prompted a change in his attitude. He had commenced the war with a limited goal—to force the rebellious Southern states back into the Union—but now, after so much anguishing deliberation, he had come to realize that slavery must become a casualty of this great civil war. As Barbara J. Fields suggests, Lincoln's government "discovered that it could not accomplish its narrow goal—union—without adopting the slaves' nobler one—universal emancipation."[24] Perhaps he still believed, as the year ended, that slavery could be gradually phased out rather than uprooted with a single stroke of his pen, but he surely knew that it would have to be abolished before the war ended. As Lincoln had predicted in 1858, a divided house cannot stand; his country could not survive half slave and half free. His God willed otherwise.

FIVE

Lincoln's War, 1863–65:
"A New Birth of Freedom"

KARL MARX, covering the American Civil War for a European news-paper, wrote that Abraham Lincoln's Emancipation Proclamation re-sembled an "ordinary summons, sent by one lawyer to another."[1] Most twentieth-century commentators on the document that initiated the emancipation of American slaves have been no kinder than Marx. One of Lincoln's foremost modern critics, Lerone Bennett Jr., calls the Emancipation Proclamation "cold, forbidding, with all the moral gran-deur of a real estate deed"; it "contains not one quotable sentence."[2] Even scholars who find Lincoln admirable have judged the proclama-tion dreary in style. David Herbert Donald states that the document "lacked the memorable rhetoric of his most notable utterances."[3] Ben-jamin Quarles comments on the proclamation's "dry, matter-of-fact style and its lack of any exalted sentiment, as if Lincoln's heart were not in it."[4] Mark E. Neely Jr. considers it "a document as dismally written as the preliminary one."[5] And according to Richard Hofstadter, "The Emancipation Proclamation of January 1, 1863 had all the moral grandeur of a bill of lading. It contained no indictment of slavery, but simply based emancipation on 'military necessity.'"[6]

The Emancipation Proclamation was a cautiously worded and, in some ways, conservative document. It emphatically identified as its authority the power vested in the president "as Commander-in-Chief, of the Army and Navy of the United States in time of actual armed rebellion against authority and government of the United States, and as a fit and necessary war measure for suppressing said rebellion" (6:29). It freed the slaves only in the sections of states in rebellion against the Union that were not, on January 1, 1863, controlled by the Union army. It defended this limited emancipation as an "act, sincerely believed to be an act of justice, warranted by the Constitution, upon military necessity" (6:30). In that sense, as Garry Wills asserts, the proclamation's author "was restricting himself, as a military leader, to the view of slaves as *property* that the Southerners themselves professed."[7] And the Emancipation Proclamation contains none of the soaring rhetoric for which its author is known.

Scholars have speculated why Lincoln chose to articulate the most dramatic action of his presidency in such deadened language. Perhaps, as Quarles suggests, Lincoln's heart was not fully in it; perhaps he was still, in 1863, a reluctant abolitionist, a man whose mind remained a divided house on the issue of slavery. In his "I See the Promised Land" speech, Martin Luther King Jr. calls Lincoln "a vacillating president" who had "finally come to the conclusion that he had to sign the Emancipation Proclamation."[8] Richard N. Current reports that Lincoln signed the bill with a "quavering hand," which might have indicated some nervousness or indecision about the document.[9] Or perhaps, as Neely suggests, Lincoln was "too worried about his potential domestic critics to unleash the full powers of his language. His purpose in that document was to calm fears, anticipate critics, and frustrate those who might doubt its constitutionality."[10] Perhaps, as Phillip Shaw Paludan argues, the "language of the great deed had to be a lawyer's language because Lincoln was taking legal action," that "when he assumed his role as enforcer of the laws Lincoln spoke as a lawyer."[11] Possibly his use of legal language, rather than his characteristically soaring rhetoric, in the Emancipation Proclamation reflects Lincoln's attempt to distance himself from the document and its bold abolitionist stroke, to identify the act as a necessary legal measure for the nation rather than an action of personal preference.

Lincoln scholars have also debated the effect of the Emancipation Proclamation. Did it really free the slaves? Barbara J. Fields thinks not. Fields believes that "at the moment of its issuance, the final Emanci-

pation Proclamation freed not a single slave who was not already entitled to freedom by an act of Congress," such as the Confiscation Acts
of 1862.[12] Current states that Lincoln's proclamation left "the slaves
untouched in the places where he had the ability to free them [in the
loyal slave states and in the sections of rebellious states that the
Union army controlled], and he was offering liberty only to those he
had no power to reach."[13] But not all historians and Lincoln scholars
agree with these assessments. Stephen B. Oates argues that Lincoln's
decree "went further than anything Congress had done," and Paludan
estimates that the Emancipation Proclamation actually freed 74 percent of American slaves.[14] George Anastaplo maintains that the Emancipation Proclamation "did work—in that it promoted the flight of
slaves from the South, in that it undermined not only the economy
but also the moral standing of the South both at home and in Europe,
and in that it contributed a significant military force of freed slaves."[15]

Oates and other Lincoln scholars also stress, quite correctly, that
the Emancipation Proclamation, besides freeing at least some of the
slaves, freed Lincoln: "For in the process of granting freedom to the
slaves, Lincoln also emancipated himself from his old dilemma. His
Proclamation now brought the private and the public Lincoln together."[16] No longer would Lincoln have to distinguish between his
personal preference that all Americans be free and his duty, as up-
holder of the Constitution and defender of the rights of slave states,
not to interfere with slavery where it already existed. After January 1,
1863, his personal preference and his professional duty were united,
one and the same. Emancipation also became joined with preservation
of the Union as the primary goals of the war. James M. McPherson
states that after the issuance of the Emancipation Proclamation, "the
abolition of slavery became an end as well as a means, a war aim virtually inseparable from Union itself."[17] Quarles asserts that the Emancipation Proclamation, originally conceived as a military measure,
"almost in spite of its creator, changed the whole tone and character
of the war."[18] After January 1, 1863, the conflict, begun at Fort Sumter
in 1861, became, fundamentally, a war to uproot American slavery.

The Emancipation Proclamation also signaled new directions in
Lincoln's thinking about race. The final Emancipation Proclamation,

unlike the preliminary proclamation of the previous September, contained no mention of gradual or compensated emancipation or colonization. In place of those proposals was a new War Department policy: "And I further declare and make known, that such persons [freed by the proclamation] of suitable condition, will be received into the armed service of the United States to garrison forts, positions, stations, and other places, and to man vessels of all sorts in said service" (6:30). So Lincoln, in a sense, was trading colonization for service in the armed forces—essentially telling freed slaves and African American freemen that if they would join the Union cause they could remain in the Union after the war. He was, according to Allen C. Guelzo, "granting African Americans a stake in the preservation of the Union, and from there it would be nearly impossible to deny men who had risked their lives for that Union the reward of full civil rights in it."[19]

Lincoln immediately began to redefine the war. A month after he issued the Emancipation Proclamation, Lincoln responded to a declaration of support for it published by workingmen of London in the *London Daily News.* In his short response, Lincoln defined the war not in terms of Union but in terms of human freedom: "It seems to have developed upon them [the American people] to test whether a government, established on the principle of human freedom, can be maintained against an effort to build one upon the exclusive foundation of human bondage" (6:88–89). For Lincoln, the war was now a test of whether the government on the American continent would be dedicated to preserving human freedom or to protecting a system built on human bondage.

This idea would, of course, receive its most eloquent expression later that year at Gettysburg. In the first sentence of the Gettysburg Address, Lincoln identified the Declaration of Independence, whose central premise extols the equality of all men, as the founding document of the American republic: "Four score and seven years ago our fathers brought forth on this continent, a new nation, conceived in Liberty, and dedicated to the proposition that 'all men are created equal'" (7:23). Scholars who have closely analyzed the address have commented on how Lincoln subtly changed Thomas Jefferson's terminology.[20] For Jefferson, the notion that all men are created equal was a self-evident truth; for Lincoln, however, that concept of equality was a proposition, one that would be tested during the history of the Republic and, most immediately, by the current civil war: "Now we are engaged in a great civil war, testing whether that nation, or any nation so conceived, and so dedicated, can long endure" (7:23). The men who "gave their lives" at Gettysburg died not solely to restore the Union but to ensure "that that nation might live" (7:23)—so that the nation dedicated to human equality might survive the terrible crucible through which it was then passing.

Lincoln was not casting aside his earlier stated war goals. The North, in his view, was still fighting to reunify the nation and to uphold the principle of popular government. The cause of the men who fought at Gettysburg—the cause to which the rest of the nation must remain dedicated—was "that government of the people, by the people, for the people shall not perish from the earth" (7:23). But Lincoln, after the implementation of the Emancipation Proclamation, was expanding the goals of the war to include abolition; his final sentence in the Gettysburg Address promised "that this nation, under God, shall have a new birth of freedom" (7:23). Donald has examined the immediate reaction to Lincoln's Gettysburg Address in the nation's newspapers and finds a good deal of criticism of Lincoln's attempt to redefine the war as a conflict over the concept of equality. According to Donald, "The bitterness of these protests was evidence that Lincoln had succeeded in broadening the aims of the war from Union to Equality and Union."[21]

Criticism of Lincoln's new war aim actually began well before he spoke at Gettysburg cemetery. Many Northerners voiced their protests when Lincoln issued the Preliminary Emancipation Proclamation— because they strongly sensed that the North, from that point on, would be fighting a war to abolish slavery. The Republicans were hit hard in the elections of November 1862, mainly due to Lincoln's promise to free the slaves on January 1, 1863. After the Emancipation Proclamation became valid, state legislatures in Indiana and Illinois protested Lincoln's decree by calling for an armistice with the South and a repeal of the Emancipation Proclamation. Desertions in the Union army were widespread. All but a few dozen men of the 128th

Illinois regiment quit the service in an act of protest against the Emancipation Proclamation. And Lincoln was crucified by the nonabolitionist press. One Ohio editor called Lincoln a "half-witted usurper" and labeled his proclamation a "monstrous, impudent, and heinous" document, "insulting to God as to man" for declaring "those 'equal' whom God created unequal."[22]

But Lincoln would not backtrack on his commitment to emancipation. In a letter to General John McClernand, written a week after the proclamation took effect, Lincoln stated that he had "authorized this struggle" against the rebellious states primarily to hold together the Union, and "I seek neither more nor less now. Still, to use a coarse, but an expressive figure, broken eggs can not be mended. I have issued the emancipation proclamation, and I cannot retract it" (6:48). On July 31, 1863, Lincoln wrote to General Stephen Hurlbut regarding William K. Sebastian, a former senator from Arkansas who had expressed a desire to return to the United States Senate. "The emancipation proclamation applies to Arkansas," Lincoln flatly told Hurlbut to inform Sebastian. "I think it is valid in law, and will be so held by the courts. I think I shall not retract or repudiate it. Those who shall have tasted actual freedom I believe can never be slaves, or quasi slaves again" (6:358). On August 26, 1863, Lincoln wrote to his friend from Illinois James Cook Conkling and declared his continued support for emancipation:

> But the proclamation, as law, either is valid, or is not valid. If it is valid, it needs no retraction. If it is valid, it can not be retracted, any more than the dead can be brought to life. Some of you profess to think its retraction would operate favorably for the Union. Why better *after* the retraction, than *before* the issue? There was more than a year and a half of trial to suppress the rebellion before the proclamation issued, the last one hundred days of which passed under an explicit notice that it was coming, unless averted by those in revolt, returning to their allegiance. The war has certainly progressed as favorably for us, since the issue of the proclamation as before. (6:408)

To ensure the legal validity of the Emancipation Proclamation, Lincoln moved to give it the force of a constitutional amendment. In June

1863, he announced his support for an amendment to the Missouri state constitution for gradual emancipation. (Lincoln still believed then that *"gradual* can be made better than *immediate* for both black and white, except when military necessity changes the case" [6:291].) The following year, he supported the effort in Maryland to amend the state constitution to abolish slavery. When Henry W. Hoffman, chair of the Maryland Unconditional Union Central Committee, requested a comment from Lincoln on Maryland's efforts, he asserted his unqualified support: "It needs not be a secret, and I presume it is no secret, that I wish success to this provision [emancipation]. I desire it on every consideration. I wish all men to be free. I wish the material prosperity of the already free which I feel sure the extinction of slavery would bring. I wish to see, in process of disappearing, the only thing which ever could bring this nation to civil war" (8:41).

Lincoln was concerned, however, that the Supreme Court might at some time in the future declare the Emancipation Proclamation unconstitutional—a violation of the right–to-property clause of the Fifth Amendment—so he gave his support for a Thirteenth Amendment to the United States Constitution that would ban slavery forever. In April 1864, the measure was passed in the Senate but failed to garner the necessary two-thirds votes in the House of Representatives. But Lincoln persisted. In June 1864, when the Republican Party, at its presidential nominating convention in Baltimore, selected Lincoln as its candidate for the November election, Lincoln announced his support for the party's platform plank advocating the passage of the Thirteenth Amendment. Such an amendment, stated Lincoln, must become "a fitting, and necessary conclusion to the final success of the Union cause" (7:380).

After his reelection, Lincoln urged reluctant members of the House to reconsider their votes against the amendment. On December 6, 1864, a month after the election, in his annual message to Congress, Lincoln told members of the House who had voted against the Thirteenth Amendment to give it their endorsement, because the American people had expressed their support for emancipation in the November election:

It is not claimed that the election has imposed a duty on members to change their views or their votes. . . . It is the voice of the people now, for the first time, heard upon the question. In a great national crisis, like ours, unanimity of action among those seeking a common end is very desirable—almost indispensable. And yet no approach to such unanimity is attainable, unless some deference shall be paid to the will of the majority. In this case the common end is the maintenance of the Union; and, among the means to secure that end, such will, through the election, is most clearly declared in favor of such constitutional amendment. (8:149)

On January 31, 1865, before the newly elected Congress took office, the House passed the Thirteenth Amendment by the necessary two-thirds vote.

On February 1, 1865, Lincoln, though he was not constitutionally required to do so, signed a congressional resolution supporting a Thirteenth Amendment to the United States Constitution consisting of two sentences:

Section 1. Neither slavery nor involuntary servitude, except as a punishment for crime whereof the party shall have been duly convicted, shall exist within the United States, or any place subject to their jurisdiction.

Section 2. Congress shall have the power to enforce this article by appropriate legislation. (8:253)

The amendment still required passage by three-quarters of the state legislatures—which would not occur until after the war—but Lincoln had helped steer the amendment through Congress. Hofstadter maintains that Lincoln's reputation as the emancipator of American slaves "rests more justly on his behind-the-scenes activity for the thirteenth amendment than on the Proclamation itself."[23]

The passage of the Thirteenth Amendment would have little effect, however, if the North did not win the war. Slavery would remain in the South as long as its generals could hold back the advancing Union armies. Thousands of slaves did leave their plantations during the war, and after January 1, 1863, they received protection from the Union army. The Fugitive Slave Law was now void; these slaves were, at least by Lincoln's decree, forever free. But through 1864, the outcome of the war was still very much in doubt. The Confederate armies fought on persistently. The Emancipation Proclamation might have liberated Lincoln, as some scholars suggest, but it alone could not end American slavery. Union victories on the battlefield would be needed to accomplish that goal.

Perhaps more immediately important to the slaves' cause than Lincoln's emancipation decree was his decision to allow African Americans to join the Union army. That policy change not only provided the North with a fresh influx of recruits at a vital time in the conflict, but it also profoundly impacted the attitude of many Northerners, Lincoln included, on issues of race. When a black man donned the Union uniform, he was no longer a slave or a freeman marked for colonization in a distant continent; he was a United States soldier fighting for his country. As Oates suggests, "A black soldier, dressed in Union blue and armed with a rifle and bayonet, posed a radically different picture from the obsequious 'Sambo' image cultivated and cherished by southern whites." According to Oates, when African Americans joined the Union army, they "undermined the whole nineteenth-century notion of Negro inferiority."[24] And Lincoln was quick to grasp the long-term implications of his decision to enlist black soldiers.

But Lincoln had not acted on a moral impulse; he had not suddenly decided, when he drafted the section of the Emancipation Proclamation concerning the recruitment of African American troops, to extend one of the basic rights and responsibilities of citizenship to black Americans. His action, like emancipation itself, was a war measure, born of necessity—perhaps desperation—not a civil rights initiative. The Union army had suffered horrendous losses during the final months of 1862. In three days of fighting at the end of August, at Bull Run, the Army of the Potomac suffered 16,000 casualties. At Antietam in September, that same army incurred more than 12,400 casualties in a single day of fierce fighting. In December, a series of suicidal charges made by that army against Confederate troops defending the hills outside of Fredericksburg, Virginia, resulted in more than 12,500 casualties. Thousands more deserted during the three months after Lincoln issued the Preliminary Emancipation Proclamation. In late 1862, more than 100,000 soldiers of the 900,000-man Union army were recorded absent without official leave.[25] Moreover, Federal generals kept over-estimating the size of Confederate armies and demanding additional troops. Lincoln invited African Americans to join the Union army on January 1, 1863, because he desperately needed more men to fight the war.

Within weeks after the issuance of the Emancipation Proclamation, African American soldiers took the field, and official reports verified that they fought as well as any Union troops. Colonel Thomas Wentworth Higginson, a white Massachusetts abolitionist, began training a regiment of black soldiers—all former slaves—in November 1862 in South Carolina. Soon after Lincoln signed the Emancipation Proclamation, Higginson led his men on an expedition by boat along the St. Mary's River on the border of Georgia and Florida. His official report of a skirmish testified to the courage and discipline of African American soldiers:

> The men have been repeatedly under fire; have had infantry, cavalry, and even artillery arrayed against them, and have in every instance come off not only with unblemished honor, but with undisputed triumph. . . .
>
> Nobody knows anything about these men who has not seen them in battle. I find that I myself knew nothing. There is a fiery energy about them beyond anything which I have ever read, except it be the French Zouaves. It requires the strictest discipline to hold them in hand. During our first attack on the river, before I had got them all penned below, they crowded at the open ends of the steamer, loading and firing with inconceivable rapidity, and shouting to each other, "Never give it up." When collected into the hold they actually fought each other for places at the few port-holes from which they could fire on the enemy.[26]

In March 1863, Higginson's men helped capture Jacksonville, Florida. At the end of April, General David Hunter, commander of the Department of the South, which included South Carolina, Georgia, and Florida, wrote to Lincoln's secretary of war, Edwin Stanton, of his African American troops: "I find the colored regiments hardy, generous, temperate, strictly obedient, possessing remarkable aptitude for military training, and deeply imbued with . . . religious sentiment. . . . I believe them capable of courage and persistence of purpose which must in the end extort both victory and admiration."[27]

Lincoln was obsessed with the daily battle news. Each day, he walked from the White House to the War Department to read battle-field reports with Secretary Stanton. Lincoln undoubtedly knew of Higginson's activities in Florida early in 1863, and he began to speak enthusiastically about recruiting additional African American soldiers. On March 26, 1863, Lincoln wrote to Military Governor Andrew Johnson of occupied Tennessee, urging Johnson to recruit a regiment of African American troops. "The colored population is the great *available* and yet *unavailed* of, force for restoring the Union," wrote Lincoln. "The bare sight of fifty thousand armed and drilled black soldiers on the banks of the Mississippi, would end the rebellion at once" (6:149–50). Lincoln's comment to Johnson reveals that he was beginning to see the black soldier equal to, perhaps even superior to, the white soldier.

On May 27, 1863, African American troops participated in their first major battle, an attack on Port Hudson, a Confederate battery on the lower Mississippi River. The attack, part of General Nathaniel P. Banks's operations in Louisiana, included two colored regiments comprising former Louisiana slaves and African American freemen from New Orleans. The Confederates beat back the Federal assault, but the African American troops distinguished themselves in combat. General Banks's official report of the battle included a comment on his African American regiments: "[T]he government will find in this class of troops effective supporters and defenders. The severe test to which they were subjected, and the determined manner in which they encountered the enemy, leaves upon my mind no doubt of their ultimate success."[28]

Eleven days later, two different African American regiments helped repulse a Confederate attack at Milliken's Bend, a Union outpost on the Mississippi River near Vicksburg. Charles Dana, an assistant secretary of war, arrived at Milliken's Bend a few days later to report on the progress of Grant's campaign. Dana wrote to his superior, Secretary of War Stanton, about the performance of black Union soldiers: "[T]he bravery of the blacks in the battle at Milliken's Bend completely revolutionized the sentiment of the army with regard to the employment of negro troops. I heard prominent officers who formerly in private had sneered at the idea of the negroes fighting express themselves after that as heartily in favor of it."[29] Lincoln's decision to enlist African Americans was producing better-than-expected results, and fresh black recruits were pouring into the Union army by the thousands.

The battle that solidified the reputation of African American troops occurred on July 18, 1863, two weeks after the Battle of Gettysburg, at Fort Wagner, on Morris Island off the South Carolina coast. (The event was memorialized in the splendid 1989 feature film *Glory*.) The 54th Massachusetts, commanded by Colonel Robert Gould Shaw, the son of prominent white Boston abolitionists, led the attack on the well-fortified Confederate installation. The assault, into the teeth of rebel cannon and rifle fire, was ill-conceived, almost suicidal. Forty percent of the 54th Massachusetts were killed, wounded, or captured in the attack. When an order to retreat was issued, Sergeant William Carney grabbed the regimental flag and returned to the Union lines—despite bullets in his head, chest, arm, and leg. Colonel Shaw was killed in the attack. After the battle, a delegation of Union soldiers under a flag of truce requested Colonel Shaw's body, but the Confederates reported that they had buried him "with his niggers." When Shaw's father heard that his son's body would not be sent home for interment, he commented to the press on the burial: "The poor, benighted wretches thought they were heaping indignities upon his dead body; but the act recoils upon them. . . . They buried him with his brave, devoted followers who fell over him and around him. . . . We can imagine no holier place than that in which he is . . . nor wish him better company—what a bodyguard he has!"[30] The story of Shaw and the 54th Massachusetts was widely reported in newspapers throughout the North. The entire Union was gradually becoming aware of the courage and prowess of African American soldiers.

Lincoln was both impressed and moved by the heroism of African American troops. He also became concerned about reports relayed to him, after the engagement at Fort Wagner, asserting that African American soldiers captured in battle were being sold into slavery or summarily executed. To deal with that problem, Lincoln, on July 30, 1863, issued an Order of Retaliation. He opened his order by asserting the essential equality of all soldiers and the unwritten code of war mandating respect for prisoners:

> It is the duty of every government to give protection to its citizens, of whatever class, color, or condition, and especially to those who are duly organized as soldiers in the public service. The law of nations and the usages and customs of war as carried on by civilized powers, permit no distinction as to color in the treatment of prisoners of war as public enemies. To sell or enslave any captured person, on account of his color, and for no offence against the laws of war, is a relapse into barbarism and a crime against civilization. (6:357)

Lincoln added that the "government of the United States will give the same protection to all its soldiers"; hence, for every Union soldier executed "in violation of the laws of war," a rebel prisoner will be executed, and for every Union soldier sent into slavery, a Confederate captive will be "placed at hard labor on the public works" (6:357).[31]

The order reveals much about the changes in Lincoln's thinking on race wrought by the war. In this order, Lincoln, who had on numerous occasions before the war asserted the superiority of the white race, suggested that white soldiers and black soldiers must be treated equally. If they must be treated equally, they must be, in Lincoln's logical mind, equals. But Lincoln did not limit the concept of equal protection to soldiers at war. In the order's opening sentence, he claimed that governments had a "duty" to "give protection" to all citizens, regardless or class, color, or condition. Here is the seed of the equal protection clause of the Fourteenth Amendment (enacted in 1868), which guarantees all United States citizens "equal protection of the laws." Perhaps Senator Charles Sumner of Massachusetts picked up on Lincoln's idea when, early in 1864, he advocated an emancipation amendment to the Constitution that included the clause, "all persons are equal before the law, so that no person can hold another as a slave."[32]

Lincoln took other steps to ensure equal treatment for all Union soldiers. He moved to equalize the pay of white and black soldiers. He also acted to meet their spiritual needs. On August 21, 1863, Lincoln met with a group of African American clergymen who wished to travel to military installations to minister to black soldiers. In his letter of passage for the ministers, Lincoln stated that their "object is a worthy one" and recommended appropriate facilities for their religious activities (6:401). Lincoln realized that African American troops, like their white comrades, might benefit from the services of the clergy during time of war, and he acted to make that possible.

Several months into 1863, Lincoln seemed certain that his policy for recruiting black troops had succeeded to a great degree, but he desired, for the sake of confirmation, the assessment of his most trusted general, Ulysses S. Grant. On August 9, 1863, he wrote to Grant to inquire about Grant's current operations in Alabama but also to share with the general his own views on the recruitment of African American soldiers:

> A word upon another subject. Gen. Thomas has gone again to the Mississippi Valley, with the view of raising colored troops. I have no reason to doubt that you are doing what you reasonably can upon the same subject. I believe it is a resource which, if vigorously applied now, will soon close the contest. It works doubly, weakening the enemy and strengthening us. . . .
>
> Mr. Dana understands you as believing that the emancipation has helped some in your military operations. I am very glad if this is so. (6:374)

In this letter to Grant, Lincoln is subtly probing for Grant's assessment of the performance of African American troops in the field. General Thomas and Charles Dana have already weighed in on the subject, but what did Grant think? The commander in chief needed the opinion of his most trusted general.

On August 23, Grant replied to Lincoln's letter, providing the president with the confirmation that he needed: "I have given the subject of arming the negro my hearty support. This, with the emancipation of the Negro, is the heavyest blow yet given the Confederacy."[33] After explaining to Lincoln some of the technical difficulties that he was encountering recruiting freed slaves, Grant offered his unqualified support for Lincoln's policy:

Gen. Thomas is now with me and you may rely on it I will give him all the aid in my power [to recruit African American soldiers]. I would do this whether the arming [of] the Negro seemed to me a wise policy or not, because it is an order that I am bound to obey and do not feel that in my position I have a right to question any policy of the Government. In this particular instance there is no objection however to my expressing an honest conviction. That is, by arming the Negro we have added a powerful ally. They will make good soldiers and taking them from the enemy weaken him in the same proportion they strengthen us. I am therefore most decidedly in favor of pushing this policy to the enlistment of a force sufficient to hold all the South falling into our hands and to aid in capturing more.[34]

As soon as he received Grant's reply, Lincoln wrote a lengthy letter to his friend James Cook Conkling of Illinois, who, with other Illinois supporters of Lincoln, was critical of the emancipation and the decision to arm the African Americans. Lincoln's letter, which was printed in many Northern newspapers, defended both decisions and signaled the continuing change in his racial attitudes. He reiterated his view that emancipation was a necessary war measure:

You dislike the emancipation proclamation; and, perhaps, would have it retracted. You say it is unconstitutional—I think differently. I think the constitution invests its commander-in-chief, with the law of war, in time of war. The most that can be said, if so much, is, that slaves are property. Is there—has there ever been—any question that by the law of war, property, both of enemies and friends, may be taken when needed? And is it not needed whenever taking it, helps us, or hurts the enemy? Armies, the world over, destroy enemies' property when they can not use it; and even destroy their own to keep it from the enemy. (6:408)

Quoting Grant (though correcting Grant's "heaveyest" to "heaviest"), Lincoln defended his recruitment of African American troops:

I know as fully as one can know the opinions of others, that some of the commanders of our armies in the field who have given us our most important successes, believe the emancipation policy, and the use of colored troops, constitute the heaviest blow yet dealt to the rebellion; and that, one of those important successes, could not have been achieved when it was, but for the aid of black soldiers. . . . I submit these opinions as being entitled to some weight against the objections, often urged, that emancipation, and arming the blacks, are unwise as military measures, and were not adopted, as such, in good faith. (6:408–9)

Then, saluting the patriotism and integrity of black soldiers, Lincoln stated, "You say you will not fight to free negroes. Some of them seem willing to fight for you; but, no matter. Fight you, then, exclusively to save the Union" (6:409).

Lincoln linked service in the Union army with emancipation: "But negroes, like other people, act upon motives. Why should they do any thing for us, if we will do nothing for them? If they stake their lives for us, they must be prompted by the strongest motive—even the promise of freedom. And the promise being made, must be kept" (6:409). Significantly, the original draft of the letter to Conkling contained the sentence, "But negroes, like other people, are creatures of motives" (6:409). Lincoln replaced "are creatures of motives" with "act upon motives" (6:409). His initial impulse had been to revert to the animal imagery that he used so often before the war when he spoke or wrote about African Americans. But upon reconsideration, Lincoln struck the word "creatures" from the sentence, subtly signaling his new way of viewing black people. Lincoln's new view of African Americans—at least those enlisted in the Union army—is also evident in the letter's penultimate paragraph:

> Peace does not appear so distant as it did. I hope it will come soon, and come to stay; and so come as to be worth the keeping in all future time. . . . And then, there will be some black men who can remember that, with silent tongue, and clenched teeth, and steady eye, and well-poised bayonet, they have helped mankind on this great consummation; while, I fear, there will be some white ones, unable to forget that, with malignant heart, and deceitful speech, they have strove to hinder it. (6:410)

For Lincoln, black men were no longer creatures, or fish on a trot-line, or cattle; they were not the bumbling Sambo characters of so much

American folklore; they were no longer a problem best remedied by exportation to some distant continent; they were not individuals labeled unfit for military service. With silent tongue, and clenched teeth, and steady eye, and well-poised bayonet, they were American warriors fighting gallantly for the Union cause.

In his annual message to Congress in December 1863, Lincoln repeated his earlier evaluations of African American troops. By that time, more than one hundred thousand African Americans had joined the Union army, and Lincoln informed Congress of their performance: "So far as tested, it is difficult to say they are not as good soldiers as any" (7:50). And Lincoln could later use the African American support for the Union war effort as an argument not to retreat on emancipation. He could not send good soldiers back into slavery after the war's end.

Given this evolution in Lincoln's racial mind-set, how could he continue to hold fast to his prewar belief that black Americans must remain socially and politically inferior to whites? Lincoln, a man of reason and logic, could not remain a white supremacist very long; racial prejudice was not rusted into Lincoln's character. In a letter written to General James Wadsworth in early 1864, Lincoln took the bold step of signaling his support for voting rights for male citizens of color. Lincoln explained to Wadsworth that one of the conditions to ending the war might be a general amnesty for those who supported the Confederate cause. "I cannot see, if universal amnesty is granted, how, under the circumstances, I can avoid exacting in return universal suffrage, or, at least, suffrage on the basis of intelligence and military service," wrote Lincoln (7:101). Then he indicated a serious commitment to improving the lot of African Americans in the United States, which would probably include the extension of voting rights:

> How to better the condition of the colored race has long been a study
> which has attracted my serious and careful attention; hence I think I am
> clear and decided as to what course I shall pursue in the premises, re-
> garding it a religious duty, as the nation's guardian of these people, who
> have so heroically vindicated their manhood on the battle-field, where,
> in assisting to save the life of the Republic, they have demonstrated in

blood their right to the ballot, which is but the humane protection of the flag they have so fearlessly defended. (7:101)

Here again, Lincoln singles out those African Americans who fought for the Union as deserving of the same rights as those guaranteed to white Americans. The African American soldier had prompted a significant change in Lincoln's thinking on racial issues.

Fehrenbacher questions the authenticity of the letter to General Wadsworth.[35] No original draft of the letter exists; it was first printed in the *New York Tribune* five months after Lincoln's death and was attributed to an issue of the *Southern Advocate* that has never been located. Roy P. Basler, however, judged the letter as authentic and included it in *The Collected Works of Abraham Lincoln*.[36] Moreover, the assertions about voting made in the Wadsworth letter appear elsewhere in Lincoln's writing of the same time period. For example, on March 13, 1864, Lincoln wrote to Michael Hahn, the new free-state governor of Louisiana, concerning the "elective franchise," which would be discussed at Louisiana's forthcoming constitutional convention: "I barely suggest for your private consideration, whether some of the colored people may not be let in—as, for instance, the very intelligent, and especially those who have fought gallantly in our ranks. They would probably help, in some trying time to come, to keep the jewel of liberty within the family of freedom" (7:243). LaWanda Cox, who has examined Lincoln's Louisiana reconstruction policy in detail, states that by January 1864—the date of the Wadsworth letter— Lincoln had twice, through his cabinet members, indicated his approval for voting rights for freeborn Louisiana African Americans.[37]

At Gettysburg, Lincoln had spoken abstractly about "a new birth of freedom" to which the war would give rise. Now in early 1864, he was beginning to define that concept more concretely. It meant suffrage for at least some African Americans. And gone was any serious talk, on Lincoln's part, of colonization—which to Oates was "an eloquent silence indicating that he had concluded that Dixie's whites and liberated Negroes must somehow learn to live together."[38] In August 1863, he had written to General Banks expressing his hope that Louisiana "adopt some practical system by which the two races could gradually live themselves out of their old relation to each other, and both come out better prepared for the new" (6:365). In February 1864, he wrote to Governor John A. Andrew of Massachusetts expressing his hope that Andrew's state would "afford a permanent home within her borders, for all, or even a large number of colored persons who will come to her" (7:191). Lincoln was no longer proposing to send former slaves and African American freemen to another continent; after the war, they would become citizens of the United States and, probably, participants in the American democracy. In his annual message to Congress in 1864, Lincoln discussed Liberia, but he no longer spoke enthusiastically of any colonization plans.

Lincoln's notion of racial equality was, initially, based on the essential sameness of all soldiers. His Order of Retaliation had asserted the equality of black and white soldiers, and his talk of voting rights always stressed that African Americans who had defended the Union cause ought to receive first consideration. But the performance of African America troops in combat prompted a gradual change in Lincoln's entire thinking on racial issues. In January 1864, Lincoln wrote to Alpheus Lewis, an Arkansas cotton dealer, concerning the desire of some Arkansas planters to employ freed slaves on their plantations. Lincoln heartily approved of this effort but was concerned about how the African American laborers would treated: "I should regard such cases with great favor, and should, as the principle, treat them precisely as I would treat the same number of free white people in the same relation and condition. Whether white or black, reasonable effort should be made to give government protection" (7:145). First, he saw the need to treat soldiers of both races equally; now he was extending that notion to white and black laborers.

In May 1864, Lincoln expanded his notion of equal treatment to the wives of soldiers. On May 19, Lincoln received a visit from Mary Elizabeth Wayt Booth, the widow of Major Lionel F. Booth, a white officer who, along with many of his African American soldiers, was killed in battle at Fort Pillow, Tennessee. Mrs. Booth was concerned about the plight of the widows and orphans of black soldiers who had been killed in combat. Many African American soldiers who lost their lives at Fort Pillow had been former slaves who were never able to formally marry the women whom they called their wives; hence, these women could not legally qualify for the pensions that Congress was in the process of approving for the widows of Union servicemen killed in combat. Apparently, Mrs. Booth's appeal persuaded Lincoln. That same day, he wrote to Senator Charles Sumner of Massachusetts, known as the Senate's chief proponent of civil rights for African Americans, to encourage some action on behalf of the widows and orphans of African American soldiers: "The bearer of this is the widow of Major Booth, who fell at Fort-Pillow. She makes a point, which I think very worthy of consideration which is, widows and orphans *in fact*, of colored soldiers who fall in our service, be placed in law, the same as if their marriages were legal, so that they can have the benefit of the provisions made the widows & orphans of white soldiers. Please see & hear Mrs. Booth."[39] The widows pension bill that Congress passed in July 1864 included provisions for the widows of African American soldiers who had not formally married.[40] Thus, Lincoln, who in his Order of Retaliation had demanded equal treatment for white and black captured soldiers, now encouraged Congress to treat equally under the law the widows of white and black servicemen. As Basler suggests, Mrs. Booth's successful appeal on behalf of the widows of African American soldiers "was but one further step in the quest for justice."[41] Lincoln's decision to recruit African American troops and his subsequent demands that these servicemen be treated the same as white servicemen were triggering other civil rights initiatives.

As the war progressed, Lincoln gradually expanded his notions of equality to include all black civilians. Early in 1865, he had received reports that African American men were being forced into the Union army. Some men were reportedly tortured until they agreed to enlist. On February 7, 1865, Lincoln wrote a short and pointed letter to Lieutenant Colonel John Glenn, stationed in Kentucky, to address this issue. He stated his hope that these disturbing reports were a mistake and added: "The like must not be done by you, or any one under you. You must not force negroes any more than white men [into the Union army]" (8:266). In this letter, Lincoln was demanding that black civilians be given the same respect as white civilians by the Union army.

But the North had little difficulty in recruiting African American men into the Union's ranks. By the summer of 1864, about 150,000 African Americans had joined the Union army and navy. Their numbers and their stellar performance in combat gave Lincoln a sound reason for standing by the Emancipation Proclamation through the difficult days of the war. Having recruited African Americans soldiers with the promise of freedom, Lincoln could not negotiate away the Emancipation Proclamation in an armistice agreement, as some critics of the war were advising. In an interview in August 1864, Lincoln stated, "There have been many who have proposed to me to return to slavery the black warriors of Port Hudson & Olustee [another engagement in which black soldiers played a key role] to their masters to conciliate the South. I should be damned in time & in eternity for so doing. The world shall know that I will keep my faith to friends & enemies, come what will" (7:507).[42]

But even Lincoln's supporters were fearful that Lincoln's steadfast refusal to consider any compromise on emancipation might cost him the presidency in the election of November 1864. On September 12, 1864, however, several weeks before the election, Lincoln again made known his unwavering support for emancipation in a letter to Isaac M. Schermerhorn, the chair of a pro-Union organization in Buffalo, New York:

> Any different policy in regard to the colored man, deprives us of his help, and this is more than we can bear. We can not spare the hundred and forty or fifty thousand now serving us as soldiers, seamen, and laborers. This is not a question of sentiment or taste, but one of physical force which may be measured and estimated as horse-power and Steam-power are measured and estimated. Keep it and you can save the Union. Throw it away, and the Union goes with it. Nor is it possible for any Administration to retain the service of these people with the express or implied understanding that upon the first convenient occasion, they are to be re-enslaved. It *can* not be; and it *ought* not to be. (8:2)

In this letter, Lincoln gave both a military and a moral reason for sustaining the Emancipation Proclamation. The 150,000 African American servicemen were indispensable to the Union cause, and the breaking of any promise to them *ought* not be done.

The *"ought"* had both moral and religious connotations. A few weeks before he wrote the letter to Schermerhorn, Lincoln had composed a letter to the editor of the *Green Bay (Wisconsin) Advocate*. In that letter, which he never mailed, Lincoln made the same point that he later made to Schermerhorn—that he could not retract the promise of freedom made to African Americans after scores of thousands of them had enlisted in the Federal army. "I am sure you will not, on due reflection, say that the promise being made, must be *broken* at the first opportunity," Lincoln wrote. "I am sure you would not desire me to say, or to leave inference, that I am ready, whenever convenient, to join in re-enslaving those who shall have served us in consideration of our promise." And then he added, "As matter of morals, could such treachery by any possibility, escape the curses of Heaven, or of any good man?" (7:500).

Lincoln believed that God would punish those who broke such a solemn promise made to men held in bondage. In Lincoln's mind, God was already exacting retribution upon the country by sending upon it this dreadful war. In his proclamation for a national fast day of March 30, 1863, Lincoln had spoken like a Puritan minister scolding the nation for its past sins:

> And, inasmuch as we know that, by His divine law, nations like individuals are subjected to punishments and chastisements in the world, may we not justly fear that the awful calamity of civil war, which now desolates the land, may be a punishment, inflicted upon us, from our presumptuous sins, to the needful end of our national reformation as a whole People? We have been the recipients of the choicest bounties of Heaven. We have been preserved, these many years, in peace and prosperity. We have grown in numbers, wealth and power, as no other nation has even grown. But we have forgotten God. We have forgotten the gracious hand which preserved us in peace, and multiplied and enriched and strengthened us; and we have vainly imagined, in the deceitfulness of our hearts, that all these blessings were produced by some superior wisdom and virtue of our own. Intoxicated with unbroken success, we have become too self-sufficient to feel the necessity of redeeming and preserving grace, too proud to pray to the God that made us! (6:156)

As the war dragged on longer than anyone expected and as the casualties mounted, Lincoln was beginning to understand that his nation was passing through a test, mandated by God, as a punishment for past sins. He did not want to add a broken promise concerning emancipation to that list of national sins.

During the war, Lincoln proclaimed nine days of national fast, thanksgiving, or prayer.[43] He urged repentance; he asked God's blessings on widows and orphans; and he requested that God subdue the nation's anger and change the hearts of those rebelling against the Union and thereby shorten the war. In December 1863, Lincoln issued an announcement of Union battlefield successes in Tennessee and thanked God "for this great advancement of the national cause" (7:35). In September 1864, he proclaimed a day of prayer and thanksgiving for General William T. Sherman's capture of Atlanta and urged all American citizens "to implore the compassion and forgiveness of the Almighty, that, if consistent with His will, the existing rebellion may be speedily suppressed." He encouraged the nation to ask God "to grant to our armed defenders and the masses of the people that courage, power of resistance and endurance necessary to secure the result" and "to soften the hearts, enlighten the minds, and quicken the consciences of those in rebellion, that they may lay down their arms and speedily return to their allegiance to the United States" so that "the effusion of blood may be stayed" (7:431–32).

Lincoln's proclamations of prayer and thanksgiving reveal his continuing belief that God guided the Union's cause, that his decisions to go to war to preserve the Union and, ultimately, to free the slaves had the blessings of the Almighty. Yet he knew that the South prayed to the same God; the proclamations of Jefferson Davis and other leaders of the rebellion also asked God's blessings upon the South's cause and thanked the Almighty for Confederate victories on the battlefield. Both sides were praying to the same God for victory, yet the bloody conflict continued. In Lincoln's mind, God clearly willed the war to carry on as punishment for some national sin. Lincoln had brooded over this matter since the beginning of the conflict—trying hard to determine God's purpose in testing the nation with this terrible civil war. In the spring of 1864, as the war headed into its fourth year, Lincoln began to reach a dreadful resolution—that God was punishing both the North and South for the national sin of slavery.

Lincoln expressed that idea in a letter on April 4, 1864, to Albert G. Hodges, editor of the *Frankfort (Kentucky) Commonwealth*, who was critical of Lincoln's decisions to emancipate the slaves and enlist them in the Union army. Lincoln, summarizing in writing what he had told Hodges and other visitors several days earlier during a White House visit, explained in detail his initial war policy to fight to preserve the Union, his efforts to avoid turning the war into a conflict over slavery, and the military necessities that prompted him to free the slaves and enlist African Americans in the Union cause. He concluded the letter by refusing to take credit for any military progress that came to the North as a result of his decision to enlist black troops: "I claim not to have controlled events, but confess plainly that events have controlled me" (7:282). The Union's failure to abort the rebellion quickly forced him to make the decisions that Hodges was questioning. Then Lincoln added that all had hoped for a quicker Union victory but that God had willed differently: "If God now wills the removal of a great wrong, and wills also that we of the North as well as you of the South, shall pay fairly for our complicity in that wrong, impartial history will find therein new cause to attest and revere the justice and goodness of God" (7:282).

Lincoln had finally reached a conclusion about God's role in the great national trauma that was devastating the nation. God sent the war as punishment for the sin of slavery. Though Lincoln, under God's guidance, had freed the slaves, the war continued; God still refused to award the North the victory. The conflict continued and the blood flowed because God saw fit to punish both the North and South for their complicity in that grievous national sin. Elton Trueblood states that Lincoln "had come really to believe that God molds history and that He employs erring mortals to effect His purpose." But Lincoln did not embrace "the arrogant nationalism which assumes that God is on our side. Lincoln's concern, he said, was whether he was on God's side."[44] Reinhold Niebuhr comes to a similar conclusion about Lincoln's speculations concerning God's role in the war:

> But the chief evidence of the purity and profundity of Lincoln's sense of providence lies in his ability . . . to avoid the error of identifying provi-

dence with the cause to which the agent is committed. He resisted this temptation. Among all the statesmen of ancient and modern periods, Lincoln alone had a sense of historical meaning so high as to cast doubt on the intentions of both sides and to place the enemy into the same category of ambiguity as the nation to which his life was committed.[45]

Lincoln, unlike so many in both the North and South, could not claim, conclusively, that God defended his side in the conflict. He sensed that God was revealing to the nation some other purpose; God was punishing both combatants for their sins.

In a brief statement in December 1864, Lincoln revealed exactly what he thought of those who used religion to cloak their cause in moral authority. Two women from Tennessee requested that Lincoln release their husbands, who were Confederate prisoners of war. The women appealed to Lincoln by asserting that their husbands were religious men. Lincoln ordered the women's husbands released, but he added a comment about their religious affiliations: "You say your husband is a religious man; tell him when you meet him, that I say I am not much of a judge of religion, but that, in my opinion, the religion that sets men to rebel and fight against their government, because, as they think, that government does not sufficiently help *some* men to eat their bread on the sweat of *other* men's faces, is not the sort of religion upon which people can get to heaven" (8:155). Lincoln recorded his brief statement on paper and handed it to Noah Brooks, a journalist, under the title "The President's Last, Shortest, and Best Speech" (8:155).

As 1864 ended, Lincoln seemed resolved that God favored neither side in the conflict, that the war and bloodletting would continue into the new year, despite the impressive Union battlefield victories of the previous several months. He still hoped that the Union would persevere, yet almost four years of war had convinced him that he could not merely reassemble the Union as it had been in 1860. The new postwar Union would have to be fundamentally different from the one destroyed by the great civil war. Minimally, it would have to be a Union without slavery; it could not stand again as a house divided on that issue. The freed slaves would have to be a part of that new Union;

having fought to save it, they could not be exiled in some distant continent. To survive, Lincoln's nation would have to experience a new birth of freedom, as he asserted at Gettysburg.

The nation would have to be reshaped, as Lincoln himself had been reshaped by the agonies of civil war. According to Oates, the war had fundamentally changed Lincoln, and the momentous decree of emancipation that ultimately gave the war its definition had liberated his thinking on racial matters:

> He had come a long distance from the harassed political candidate of 1858, opposed to emancipation lest his political career be jeopardized, convinced that only the distant future could remove slavery from his troubled land, certain that only colonization could solve the ensuing problem of racial adjustment. He had also come a long way in the matter of Negro social and political rights. . . . The Proclamation had indeed liberated Abraham Lincoln, enabling him to act more consistently with his moral convictions.[46]

Fields states that the war's original goal—preserving the Union—was "too shallow to be worth the sacrifice of a single life."[47] Lincoln probably would not have completely agreed with that assertion; he had begun the war—and the sacrifice of American lives—to preserve the Union. Yet after emancipation, the war had taken on a new meaning for Lincoln; early in 1865, in his Second Inaugural Address, he would attempt to articulate that new meaning to his countrymen and countrywomen, both North and South. He would share with them the truth that he had discovered after almost four years of anguished deliberation and soul searching. He would tell a truth that he felt needed to be told.

SIX

Lincoln's Inaugural Jeremiad:
"Woe Unto the World Because of Offences!"

IN 1634, the Massachusetts Bay Colony began a tradition that became known as the election day sermon. In May, the individual Massachusetts villages sent deputies to Boston to elect the colonial governor's assistants, who with the governor would form the General Court, which would rule the colony for the next year. Election days were holidays in seventeenth-century Boston. Tourists traveled to the city from settlements miles away to watch the formal procession of political, religious, and military leaders make its way through the city streets to Boston's First Church or, after 1658, to the Boston Town House for a series of speeches and prayers. A key component of the day's ceremonies was the election sermon, delivered by a leading member of Boston's Puritan clergy, for whom offering the sermon was a great honor.

Nathaniel Hawthorne depicts a typical election day ceremony in Chapter 21 of *The Scarlet Letter*, appropriately titled "The New England Holiday." The Boston marketplace is "thronged with the craftsmen and other plebeian inhabitants of the town, in considerable numbers; among whom, likewise, were many rough figures, whose attire of deer-skins marked them as belonging to some of the forest settlements, which surrounded the little metropolis of the day." When Pearl asks Hester Prynne why all the people have taken off from work and gathered in the city, Hester explains to her daughter, "They wait to see the procession pass. . . . For the Governor and the magistrates are to go by, and the ministers, and all the great people and good people, with the music, and the soldiers marching before them." A short time later, music is heard, and the procession approaches on its way to the meetinghouse. The military escort first appears, followed by "men of civil eminence" and then Rev. Arthur Dimmesdale, "the young and eminently distinguished divine, from whose lips the religious discourse of the anniversary was expected."[1] The procession reaches the meetinghouse, and Rev. Dimmesdale enters to deliver his sermon.

The election sermon was, like most other Puritan sermons, a jeremiad, defined by Sacvan Bercovitch as "a mode of public exhortation that originated in the European pulpit, was transformed in both form and content by the New England Puritans, persisted through the eighteenth century, and helped sustain a national dream through two hundred years of turbulence and change." The American jeremiad, as delivered by the New England clergy of the seventeenth and eighteenth centuries on special public occasions, "was a ritual designed to join social criticism to spiritual renewal."[2] The typical jeremiad lamented how the community had failed to adhere to the noble Christian ideals articulated by the colony's Puritan founders and offered "a strategy for prodding the community forward" toward the goal of making those ideals real.[3] During the sermon, the minister would usually deliver some fire and brimstone upon the sinful congregation, which undoubtedly had strayed from the path of Christian righteousness. Thomas Hooker's reproof in a sermon delivered in 1640 is standard jeremiad fare:

> A word of terror to dash the hopes and sink the hearts of all haughty and hard-boiled sinners: God owns not such, will never vouchsafe his gracious presence with them or his blessing upon them for good. . . . Hear and fear then all you stout-hearted, stubborn, and rebellious creatures, whose consciences can evidence that the day is yet to dawn, the hour yet to come, that ever you found your sins a pressure to you—they have been your pastime and delight in which you have pleased yourselves. . . . The great God of heaven and earth is up in arms against thee, he is upon the march to work thy destruction. . . .[4]

Election day, marking the commencement of the new political year, offered the ministry a special opportunity to rally the community to renew the goals of the founders. According to Harry S. Stout, the minister selected to deliver the election sermon often "assumed the persona of the Old Testament prophet he quoted in his text."[5] He urged his audience to recall the special covenant that God had made with the first Puritan settlers in New England and warned that a failure to do so would bring down upon the colony God's wrath and retribution. According to A. W. Plumstead, the election sermon became "an occasion for assessment and prophecy of New England's 'errand into the wilderness,'" the "center of a ritual in which a community gave thanks and took stock." Standard themes included "a survey of Biblical ideas on government and the good ruler, a look at the good old days, a catalog of what's wrong with New England, a plea to do better, and a look at what might lie ahead."[6]

By the late eighteenth century, the election sermons had become more secular in their themes and content. They were used to condemn King George III during the American Revolution and to extol the virtues of the early American republic. In a more secular form, election sermons continued through the late nineteenth century and, in Plumstead's words, "helped shape the traditions of the Inaugural, Fourth of July orations, and State of the Union messages."[7] By Abraham Lincoln's time, the ritual had become almost completely secularized. Politicians, not clergymen, generally delivered the discourse. While the speakers still asked God's blessing upon the community, they focused on the political issues of the day rather than on the spiritual needs of the people. When American presidents, in their inaugural addresses or State of the Union speeches, assess the position of the United States in the world, chronicle the nation's strengths and weaknesses, and offer a direction toward which the country should embark to fulfill its lofty national aims, they are continuing a tradition established by Puritan ministers in the seventeenth century.

During the nineteenth century, presidential inauguration day in Washington, D.C., was very much like election day in the old Puritan colony. A parade of soldiers and civic dignitaries would approach the Capitol, the nation's meetinghouse, and gather around the podium to hear the president assess the national condition and offer some idea about the direction that the country would go during the next four years. Lincoln's second inaugural, on March 4, 1865, adhered to this tradition. Hours before the time set for Lincoln to take his oath of office, a parade commenced and moved through Washington's muddy streets toward the Capitol. The procession included police corps, fire fighters, troops (including the 45th Regiment United States Colored Troops), bands, politicians, and floats. Before Lincoln delivered his inaugural address from a platform built over the Capitol's east portico, Vice President Andrew Johnson, nursing a serious hangover, took his oath of office inside the Capitol. Johnson delivered a long, incoherent address that only historians have bothered to remember. After Johnson's speech, the presidential party moved outdoors for Lincoln to deliver his inaugural address and take his oath of office.

Garry Wills states that "Lincoln had his work cut out for him, and his audience could reasonably expect a serious engagement with matters that were haunting everyone on the eve of victory."[8] The great civil war that had enveloped the nation was coming to a close, and American citizens perhaps anticipated some comments by Lincoln on the serious problems of the day. Would the rebellious Southern states be welcomed back into the Union when the conflict ended or treated as a conquered nation? Would the Confederacy's civic and military leaders be formally charged with treason? What would become of the four million freed slaves? Would they be made United States citizens with the full rights of citizenship? These were questions on the minds of most Americans on the day of Lincoln's second inauguration.

The presidential inaugural address, however, was not usually a speech in which to articulate detailed policy proposals. In most presidential inaugural addresses prior to Lincoln's, the new president would offer only very general ideas about his administration's goals, as Andrew Jackson had done in 1829 when he outlined, in a very general way, his administration's fiscal policy:

> The management of the public revenue—that searching operation in all governments—is among the most delicate and important trusts in ours, and it will, of course, demand no inconsiderable share of my offi-

cial solicitude. Under every aspect in which it can be considered it would appear that advantage must result from the observance of a strict and faithful economy. This I shall aim at the more anxiously both because it will facilitate the extinguishments of the national debt, the unnecessary duration of which is incompatible with real independence, and because it will counteract that tendency to public and private profligacy which a profuse expenditure of money by the Government is but too apt to engender. Powerful auxiliaries to the attainment of this desirable end are to be found in the regulations provided by the wisdom of Congress for the specific appropriation of public money and the prompt accountability of public officers.[9]

Presidential inaugural addresses prior to Lincoln's generally contained these kinds of general policy announcements, along with stock statements praising the wisdom of the "Founding Fathers" and respecting the authority of the Constitution. Specific policy commitments—such as James Polk's discussion of the annexation of Texas in 1845 and James Buchanan's discussion of popular sovereignty in 1857—were actually quite rare.

But Lincoln had used his first inaugural to articulate his positions on critical issues of the day such as slavery, secession, and the Fugitive Slave Law—probably because the anxious national mood when he took office in 1861 demanded that he reveal specific policy positions. So perhaps, as Wills suggests, the nation also expected some important policy announcements on March 4, 1865, when Lincoln would take the oath of office to commence his second term. Lincoln, however, delivered something very different from what the public probably expected. He offered neither specific policy positions nor the general platitudes about American government that composed the standard menu of previous presidential inaugurals. Little is known about the composition of Lincoln's Second Inaugural Address—except that on February 26, 1865, he told some congressmen who were visiting the White House that he had written about six hundred words of it. What he was composing for delivery on inauguration day was an election jeremiad. Wills points out that at Gettysburg, Lincoln reached back to the themes of ancient Greek funeral oratory.[10] In his Second Inaugural Address, he returned to the Puritanical sermons of his youth.

Congressman Isaac N. Arnold—and many subsequent commentators—called Lincoln's Second Inaugural Address his sermon on the mount, an appropriate moniker for Lincoln's speech. Several biographers suggest that Lincoln, as a child, frequently had mimicked the fire-and-brimstone clergymen whom he heard at Sunday services;[11] in a sense, his first public speeches were jeremiads. Although he was a member of no organized religion, Lincoln knew the Bible well; as Edmund Wilson states, he had the book "at his fingertips and quoted it more often than anything else."[12] He once told a group of White House visitors who had presented him with a Bible that the book was "the best gift God has given man" (7:542). Lincoln's audience, too, knew the Bible well, and they believed in Lincoln's God—the Supreme Ruler of Nations who punished transgressions severely and who paid particular heed to the American experiment. As Alfred Kazin states, "God was not yet dead in 1865. . . . He was the presence and the destiny, the ever-living God of religious seekers and zealots, absolutists of the spirit."[13] When he approached the podium to deliver his address, Lincoln was going to tell his countrymen and countrywomen what their God thought of slavery and their war. For his biblical text, Lincoln chose a passage from the gospel of Matthew: "Woe unto the world because of offences! for it must needs be that offences come; but woe to that man by whom the offence cometh!" (Matthew 18:7). The offense was American slavery, and the ones by whom the offense came were the American people. Lincoln planned to tell his countrymen and countrywomen that they were sinners in the hands of an angry God.

Benjamin Barondess suggests that "nothing of great importance" is said in the first two paragraphs of Lincoln's address.[14] That is hardly the case. Lincoln opened by stating that he had no need to make a long address, as he did on the same occasion four years ago, because "little that is new could be presented" on "the great contest which still absorbs the attention, and engrosses the energies of the nation." The American people had spent the past four years discussing "every point and phase" of the war, and Lincoln did not feel compelled to add to that discussion (8:332). Clearly, Lincoln had a very specific point to make in this speech, and he alerted his audience, in the opening sentences, that he did not want to get lost in tangential issues that the public had already repeatedly debated during the past four years; he wanted to get right to the truth of the matter. Lincoln offered "high hope" that the war would soon conclude—"The progress of our arms . . . is, I trust, reasonably satisfactory and encouraging to all" (8:332)—but he ventured no specific prediction on that point. The war had carried on longer than either side expected, and Lincoln did not feel confident to prophesize an end to the combat.

In the second paragraph of his address, Lincoln replayed the events of 1861 that led to the present civil war:

> On the occasion corresponding to this four years ago, all thoughts were anxiously directed to an impending civil-war. All dreaded it—all sought to avert it. While the inaugural address was being delivered from this place, devoted altogether to *saving* the Union without war, insurgent agents were in the city seeking to *destroy* it without war—seeking to dissolve the Union, and divide effects, by negotiation. Both parties deprecated war; but one of them would *make* war rather than let the nation survive; and the other would *accept* war rather than let it perish. And the war came. (8:332)

Here Lincoln, at first, seemed to imply that the South was mainly responsible for initiating the great conflict that would descend upon the nation. His First Inaugural Address was devoted to saving the Union without war while insurgents were already working to destroy the Union. The rebellious Southern states would *make* war, while the North would merely *accept* it. But Lincoln quickly suggested that the great conflict was not simply a confrontation between angelic loyalists and barbarous insurrectionists. "Both parties deprecated war," and neither party, according to Lincoln, initiated combat: "And the war came." As Wills states, "Events were beyond anyone's control. War came of itself, the personified process overriding personal agents."[15]

Wills brilliantly demonstrates how Lincoln, in this second paragraph, matched his rhetoric to his message. In the first two sentences of the paragraph, Lincoln uses "all thoughts" and "all" as his subjects; "all" is also the subject of the independent clause following the first dash. The word "all" suggests a country united—all for one. The paragraph's penultimate sentence also begins with a word connoting unity—"both." The word "but" later in that sentence, however, signals a change in direction: "but one of them would *make* war rather than let the nation survive; and the other would *accept* war rather than let it perish." "All" and "both," terms suggesting unity, have given way to "one of them" and "the other," terms suggesting discord. And so the war came.[16]

According to Barondess, Lincoln ceased speaking at the start of the third paragraph: "Someone else has taken his place. It is the prophet Jeremiah, standing among the ruins of the temple of Jerusalem, casting the sins of the multitude into their faces, and calling on them for contrition and repentance."[17] Lincoln opened the third paragraph by clearly identifying the cause of this war that seemed to come of its own volition:

> One eighth of the whole population were colored slaves, not distributed generally over the Union, but localized in the Southern part of it. These slaves constituted a peculiar and powerful interest. All knew that this interest was, somehow, the cause of the war. To strengthen, perpetuate, and extend this interest was the object for which the insurgents would rend the Union, even by war; while the government claimed no right to do more than to restrict the territorial enlargement of it. (8:332)

For Lincoln, initially, the war had begun over secession, the attempt by several Southern states to rend the Union by voting to withdraw from it. He had maintained that posture—that fiction, perhaps— through the first seventeen months of the conflict. In mid-September 1862, however, he had told a delegation of Chicago Christians that slavery was the essential cause of the rebellion. Now here, in March 1865, Lincoln was making that conclusion, arrived after much anguished deliberation, known to the nation. As Ronald C. White Jr. states, "Lincoln is intimating that the North, even when it spoke of defending the Union, knew that slavery was the key moral issue underneath its political rhetoric."[18] But as William Lee Miller suggests, Lincoln's assertion that slavery had caused the war "does not have the bane of self-righteousness. It has the generous imprecision represented by that marvelous 'somehow'" in the middle of Lincoln's sentence.[19]

Slavery caused the war in some way, and Lincoln would soon explain exactly the way that it happened.

Lincoln noted, however, that neither side expected a war of such magnitude to result from the prewar disagreements between North and South over slavery: "Neither party expected for the war, the magnitude, or the duration, which it has already attained. Neither anticipated that the *cause* of the conflict might cease with, or even before, the conflict itself should cease. Each looked for an easier triumph, and a result less fundamental and astounding" (8:332–33). Lincoln was avoiding the kind of self-righteous statement that would put the blame for the long and bloody war squarely on the South's shoulders. Neither the North nor the South expected that its position on slavery would result in such prolonged bloodshed. Each side had looked for an easier resolution of the issue, and even after the war's central issue was resolved—Lincoln's Emancipation Proclamation went into effect more than two years earlier—the war, for some reason, stubbornly continued. As Lois Einhorn states, the war had come of its own volition and had a force of its own.[20]

After starting three consecutive sentences with "neither," "neither," and "each"—terms suggesting separation—Lincoln opened the next sentence with "both": "Both read the same Bible, and pray to the same God;" but "*each* invokes His aid against the other" (emphasis added). For Lincoln, this kind of prayer is illogical. If both North and South pray to the same God for victory, how can God answer the prayers of both? Lincoln then suggested that, perhaps, the South's prayer was less worthy than the North's: "It may seem strange that any men should dare ask a just God's assistance in wringing their bread from the sweat of other men's faces; but let us judge not that we be not judged" (8:333). This sentence is a variation of the statement that he had made the previous December to the Southern woman seeking the release of her husband, a Confederate soldier, from a Union prisoner-of-war camp. The woman had claimed that her husband was a religious man, and Lincoln had responded by telling the woman that he was suspicious of any religion that prompts men to rebel against their government because that government does not help some individuals to "eat their bread on the sweat" of their slaves' faces (8:155). But Lin-

coln now added, "but let us judge not that we not be judged" (8:333).
He again avoids the self-righteousness that might allow him to cen-
sure the South for religiously incorrect prayer; after four years of
bloody combat, he cannot make that kind of judgment.

Lincoln's passage contains at least two biblical allusions. In Genesis, after Adam and Eve committed sin, God tells Adam that "in the
sweat of thy face shalt thou eat bread, till thou return unto the
ground" (Genesis 3:19). Lincoln suggested that those who owned
slaves have disobeyed God's command, for they have wrung their
bread from the sweat of *other* men's faces rather than exerting their
own sweat to earn their bread. The other allusion is to Matthew's gospel, when Christ preaches the value of withholding judgment: "Judge
not, that ye not be judged. For with what judgment ye judge, ye shall
be judged: and with what measure ye mete, it shall be measured to
you again" (Matthew 7:1–2). Lincoln refused to judge the South's motives lest his own motives be judged. And he was not completely free
from sin. He, too, had tolerated slavery; until late in 1862, he had been
willing to allow it to continue indefinitely if its continuance would
preserve the Union.

Lincoln then calculated, in the next few sentences, why God answered the prayers of neither the North nor the South:

> The prayers of both could not be answered; that of neither has been an-
> swered fully. The Almighty has His own purposes. "Woe unto the world
> because of offences! for it must needs be that offences come; but woe to
> that man by whom the offence cometh!" If we shall suppose that Ameri-
> can Slavery is one of those offences which, in the providence of God,
> must needs come, but which, having continued through His appointed
> time, He now wills to remove, and that He gives to both North and
> South, this terrible war, as the woe due to those by whom the offence
> came, shall we discern therein any departure from those divine attri-
> butes which the believers in a Living God always ascribe to Him? (8:333)

Stephen B. Oates states that this passage reveals Lincoln's "apocalyptic conclusion about the nature of the war," arrived at after must anxious speculation.[21] God could not answer the prayers of either the
North or the South, Lincoln concluded, because God has his own purposes for allowing the war to continue.

Lincoln had made that same point in his Meditation on the Divine Will of September 1862 and in two letters to Eliza P. Gurney, one written on October 26, 1862, and one almost two years later, on September 4, 1864. In his private meditation on God's will, Lincoln had written, "In the present civil war it is quite possible that God's purpose is something different from the purpose of either party. . . . I am almost ready to say this is probably true—that God wills this contest, and wills that it shall not end yet" (5:404). In the first letter to Gurney, Lincoln had stated, "If I had been allowed my way this war would have been ended before this, but we find it still continues; and we must believe that He permits it for some wise purpose of his own, mysterious and unknown to us" (5:478). In the later letter, Lincoln had made a similar assertion: "The purposes of the Almighty are perfect, and must prevail, though we erring mortals may fail to accurately perceive them in advance. We hoped for a happy termination of this terrible war long before this; but God knows best, and has ruled otherwise" (7:535). But by the time Lincoln had written that second letter to Gurney, he had come to a conclusion about God's mysterious purpose. Four months earlier, he had revealed it in a letter to Albert G. Hodges, editor of the *Frankfort (Kentucky) Commonwealth*: "If God now wills the removal of a great wrong, and wills also that we of the North as well as you of the South, shall pay fairly for our complicity in that wrong, impartial history will find therein new cause to attest and revere the justice and goodness of God" (7:282).

Lincoln failed to pin the blame for the war entirely on the South. If the South were solely at fault for the four years of bloodletting, then God would have allowed the North a swifter victory. Surely God would have given the North the victory shortly after January 1, 1863, when Lincoln acted authoritatively to remove "the offense" from American soil and the war became a conflict over slavery rather than one whose sole goal was to reunite the severed nation. But God willed the conflict to continue for two more hard years, and, as he stated in the opening sentences of his address, Lincoln knew not when it might conclude. Wills notes Lincoln's use of the term "American Slavery" rather than "Southern Slavery" or simply "slavery"—suggesting that slavery was "a single offense ascribed to the whole nation. . . . There is one agent by which the offense came, . . . and that agent is the undifferentiated American people."[22]

The South had fostered slavery in its bosom, and the North had tolerated it, for various reasons. Thomas Jefferson's original draft of the Declaration of Independence charged King George III for waging "a cruel war against human nature itself, violating its most sacred right of life and liberty in the persons of a distant people who never offended him, captivating them into slavery in another hemisphere, or to incur miserable death in their transportation thither."[23] When the representatives from the Southern slaveholding colonies protested this passage, these words were struck from the Declaration. For the sake of unity against Great Britain, the Northern colonies acquiesced to the South's peculiar institution. Again for the sake of unity, the delegates at the Philadelphia Convention of 1787 chose not to create a Constitution that outlawed slavery. The Northern textile mills spun Southern cotton picked by slaves. White laborers in the border states like Indiana and Lincoln's Illinois relied on slavery to keep the blacks out, ensuring that jobs would be available for white workers and that pay scales would not fall. To preserve the Union, antislavery Northerners like Daniel Webster compromised with the slave power, passing the Fugitive Slave Law and other legislation that protected slavery.

Edmund Wilson correctly states that Lincoln had been, for some time, less than perfectly clear that God was committed to the side of the North in the war. "This line of anxious speculation," states Wilson, "is to culminate in the Second Inaugural Address."[24] Both Wills and Miller make the point that Lincoln, in the Second Inaugural, avoided the self-righteous crusading of Northerners like Julia Ward Howe, whose great anthem, "The Battle Hymn of the Republic," assured the North that God was on its side.[25] Howe's God "hath loosed the fateful lightning of his terrible swift sword" against the South; his face appeared in the watch-fires of the Union military camps. But Lincoln's God, the Puritan God of his youth, the living God who monitored the actions of nations and peoples, had unleashed his sword upon the whole nation. "Woe to that man by whom the offence cometh!" said Lincoln. The offense had come by both the North and the South, and God's woe was delivered upon both. The war was bleeding both sections of the nation evenly. Lincoln even used his rhetoric to avoid an attitude of self-righteousness. He began the sentence that identifies slavery as a national offense with "If we shall suppose," as if he were not a prophet delivering to his followers the words of God but a mere mortal struggling to find God's message in earthly events.

The biblical quote—"Woe unto the world because of offenses!"—comes from the gospel of Matthew. Christ's disciples ask him who is the greatest in the kingdom of heaven, and Christ responds by calling forth a child. "Except ye be converted, and become as little children, ye shall not enter into the kingdom of heaven," Christ tells them (Matthew 18:3). Then Christ adds, "But whoso shall offend one of these little ones which believe in me, it were better for him that a millstone were hanged about his neck, and *that* he were drowned in the depth of the sea. Woe unto the world because of offenses! for it must needs be that offenses come; but woe to that man by whom the offense cometh!" (Matthew 18:6–7). Lincoln, patronizingly, had viewed the slaves as a meek, almost childlike people; to the slaves, Lincoln was Father Abraham. By offending enslaved people, the nation had failed to heed Christ's warning about offending "these little ones," and now the nation must pay for that offense.

Lincoln followed this passage with a sentence, in the middle of his third paragraph, that momentarily abated the force of his devastating critique of his nation: "Fondly do we hope—fervently do we pray—that this mighty scourge of war may speedily pass away" (8:333). This sentence, perhaps the most poetic in the whole address, resembles—to borrow a simile from Emily Dickinson—the stillness in the air between the heaves of a storm. The previous several sentences referred to the woe that God brought down upon the nation because of the offense of slavery; the following sentence, the last in the third paragraph, would continue that point. But now, between the sentences highlighting God's vengeance, Lincoln offered a prayer that God's wrath might soon subside, that the war might speedily pass away, that it might be brought to a swift conclusion. The sentence makes another allusion, a very subtle one, to the gospel of Matthew. When Christ is in the Garden of Gethsemane on the night before he died, he prays, "O my Father, if it be possible, let this cup pass from me: nevertheless, not as I will, but as thou *wilt*. . . . O my Father, if this cup may not pass away from me, except I drink it, thy will be done" (Matthew 26: 39, 42).

In this passage, Christ, fully aware that he will suffer and die the next day for the sins of humankind, asks God if it were possible for his cup of punishment to pass from him, if some other, less terrifying fate might be substituted. Lincoln, too, asked God, "Fondly do we hope— fervently do we pray," to abate the nation's punishment, to lift from his people "this mighty scourge of war." Like Christ, however, Lincoln realized that the cup of punishment must be taken, not passed; God's will must be done: "Yet, if God wills that it [the war] continue, until all the wealth piled by the bond-man's two hundred and fifty years of unrequited toil shall be sunk, and until every drop of blood drawn with the lash, shall be paid by another drawn with the sword, as was said three thousand years ago, so still must it be said 'the judgments of the Lord, are true and righteous altogether'" (8:333). After his brief prayer for a conclusion to his nation's suffering, Lincoln continued his rhetorical storm, describing God as some heavenly accountant who has kept an exact toll of the sins piled up during slavery's reign and who now demands that the nation sink that debt by shedding its blood on the battlefields of war. And in Lincoln's view, God's harsh judgments are true and righteous—because the nation's sins have been many and grave.

Kazin calls this passage in Lincoln's address "a great public cry from the heart." Never before had Lincoln "condemned the whole system of slavery so totally, without qualification and with so much emotion."[26] Waldo Braden states that Lincoln's Second Inaugural Address featured "a milder rhetoric steeped in democratic and Christian sentiment."[27] But there is nothing mild about this passage. As Allen C. Guelzo asserts, Lincoln had come to see in the war "the most 'astounding' result imaginable, something that transcended its causes, a kind of divine weighing of the republic—not just the South, but South and North together—in which the war's losses were the wages of national sin, payable in both life and treasure."[28]

David Herbert Donald and other Lincoln scholars suggest that in this passage Lincoln was absolving both the North and South of the guilt for the war, shifting responsibility for the bloodshed to God.[29] That is hardly the case. Lincoln clearly identified slavery as a grievous national sin, an offense committed by the whole nation that would eventually merit God's woe. In Lincoln's view, God, perhaps waiting for the nation to purge itself from sin, had allowed slavery to continue. But the nation took no steps to remove the sin from its soil; slavery continued through God's appointed time. And a just and righteous God brought vengeance upon the nation in the form of a great civil war. According to Lincoln, God is not to blame for the nation's bloody trial. God, irritated by the erring mortals who compromised on slavery rather than abolish it, chose his own way to uproot slavery, and Lincoln was urging his countrymen and countrywomen to accept God's judgment.

The passage concerning God's judgment—"the judgments of the Lord, are true and righteous altogether"—is from Psalms 19:7–9:

> The law of the Lord *is* perfect, converting the soul: the testimony of the Lord *is* sure, making wise the simple.
>
> The statutes of the Lord *are* right, rejoicing the heart: the commandment of the Lord *is* pure, enlightening the eyes.
>
> The fear of the Lord *is* clean, enduring for ever: the judgments of the Lord *are* true *and* righteous altogether.

In crafting this section of his address, Lincoln drew from both the Old and the New Testaments. As Wills suggests, "Between Matthew above and the Psalmist below, Lincoln gave to his thought the sanctions of both Old and New Testaments, both of them speaking here with minatory, not exculpatory, finality."[30]

Lincoln concluded his Second Inaugural Address by advocating the New Testament notion of charity for all: "With malice toward none; with charity for all; with firmness in the right, as God gives us to see the right, let us strive on to finish the work we are in; to bind up the nation's wounds; to care for him who shall have borne the battle, and for his widow, and his orphan—to do all which may achieve and cherish a just, and a lasting peace, among ourselves, and with all nations" (8:333). Lincoln's advice came, perhaps, from Peter's first epistle: "And above all things have fervent charity among yourselves: for charity shall cover the multitude of sins" (Peter 4:8). Charity now could cover even the sin of slavery. Miller suggests that Lincoln had opened the way for charity with his remarks about judgment earlier in the speech. With judgment comes malice; without judgment, charity is possible for all.[31] Charity is also possible, as George M. Fredrickson explains, because both sides in the war are guilty: "[T]he guilt was shared by both North and South. Hence he could call for a spirit of forgiveness and moderation."[32] Moreover, the North and South had suffered equally. When both sides have suffered enough, when the nation's debt from the sin of slavery is sunk, God would end the war, and there would be no need for further bloodshed—no executions of Confederate political leaders, no imprisonment for Confederate military officers. Lincoln would not become Creon, the ruler of Thebes in Sophocles' *Antigone* who, after a civil war, ordered the bodies of those fighting against the state to lie unburied to be picked apart by buzzards and wild dogs. Lincoln would offer malice toward none.

Guelzo sees no hint of redemption in Lincoln's speech.[33] But Lincoln's last paragraph suggests otherwise. The nation had drunk from its cup of punishment, as the Christ of Matthew's gospel, humankind's redeemer, had drunk from his cup; the bloodshed would cleanse the land of the sin of slavery and open the way, Lincoln hoped, for "a just and a lasting peace, among ourselves, and with all nations." The nation, under God's guidance, would bind up its wounds, and the warring factions would forgive each other. James M. McPherson states that in the last paragraph of his address, Lincoln "invoked the New Testament lesson of forgiveness; he urged a soft peace once the war was over."[34] Wills makes a similar point. In the last paragraph of the address, Lincoln turns "from this vision of blood" and "brings redemption."[35] By ending with the hope of forgiveness and redemption, Lincoln was keeping within the tradition of the jeremiad. In the conventional American jeremiad, "God's punishments are *corrective*, not destructive," Bercovitch informs us.[36] Those harsh Puritan sermons often ended optimistically, with the hope that God would continue to bestow his grace upon his chosen community even though its sins were many.

Wills states that Lincoln's Gettysburg Address "fails to express the whole of Lincoln's mind. It must be supplemented with his other most significant address, the Second Inaugural, where *sin* is added to the picture."[37] But the Second Inaugural offers more than sin; it redefines the war, just as the Emancipation Proclamation had redefined the war two years earlier. Then later, at Gettysburg, Lincoln had paid tribute to those who fought with dedication for a noble cause. He had re-named the bloody war, calling it a task and a cause. As Wills states, at the Gettysburg battlefield, the scene four months earlier of unimagin-able human slaughter, "The tragedy of macerated bodies, the many bloody and ignoble aspects of this inconclusive encounter, are trans-formed in Lincoln's rhetoric. . . . The stakes of the three days' butchery are made intellectual, with abstract truths being vindicated."[38] On March 4, 1865, the contest between North and South was again a war. Lincoln, who had once stated that "war, at its best, is terrible" (7:394), used the term "war" only twice in his 272-word speech at Gettysburg. In the Second Inaugural, which is two and a half times the length of the Gettysburg Address, he used the word twelve times. Between the Gettysburg Address and the Second Inaugural were sixteen months of bitter fighting—Kennesaw Mountain, Cold Harbor, the Wilderness, Sherman's March to Sea. The noble cause to which Lincoln urged ded-ication at Gettysburg had become a national bloodbath, one that, ac-cording to Lincoln, only God could have sent as punishment for some grave sin. At Gettysburg, Lincoln referred vaguely to completing the nation's "unfinished work" (7:23). Now Lincoln realized that the war was not the nation's work but God's work, whose completion he could not predict.

Both Donald and Einhorn consider the Second Inaugural Address to be an impersonal speech because Lincoln used only two first-person singular pronouns—"myself" and "I"—which appear in the opening paragraph.[39] Pronouns notwithstanding, the address reveals much about Lincoln; it makes public the significant changes that took place in the man during more than twenty years of public life. Early in his career, in 1848, Lincoln had identified himself as an Illinois man who "did not keep so constantly thinking about" slavery (2:3). He had gen-erally opposed slavery, but he had taken no active role in abolishing it; he had hoped that emancipation would come some day in the distant

future. For the most part, he had avoided the most pressing political
and moral problem facing his nation until 1854, when the passage of
the Kansas-Nebraska Act threatened to bring slavery into the Northern free territories. He had campaigned for the Senate, in 1858, on a
policy of noninterference with slavery, and he had entered the White
House, more than two years later, holding fast to that position. As
president, he had pushed for a gradual, compensated emancipation,
which was simply another plan to extend slavery's life. Almost in desperation, he had, in 1863, issued the Emancipation Proclamation, freeing slaves in certain designated areas of the country. Eventually he had
seen that what he had predicted in his House Divided speech of 1858
was true: The nation could not stand half slave and half free. So he
had supported a constitutional amendment to ban slavery forever from
United States soil. Now he was informing the nation that it had
sinned, that those who had for so long embraced and tolerated slavery,
himself included, had offended God. He was telling Americans that
their sin was no minor offense, that it was one that merited severe
retribution from the just and living God who monitored the nation's
progress, and that the nation's terrible civil war was its deserved punishment for that sin.

Lincoln's Second Inaugural Address also revealed much about its
author's religious growth. William J. Wolf calls the speech "the climax
of Lincoln's religious development."[40] As a young man, he had been,
in matters of faith, the typical Victorian brooder. His friends and the
authors whom he read had been religious skeptics. He once had been
forced to deny publicly a charge of religious infidelity. As he arrived at
middle age, however, he had reached back to find the Puritan God of
his youth. After Lincoln had entered the White House, that God had
become, for Lincoln, the living God of history who directed the affairs
of humankind. Lincoln had been certain that this God abhorred slavery and sustained the Union's cause. But as the war dragged on, Lincoln, after much deliberation, had perceived some other, mysterious
motive on God's part for allowing the war to continue. Now he saw
God's motive clearly, and he announced his frightening conclusion to
the nation in his Second Inaugural Address.

Lincoln had moved, too, on issues concerning race. Early in his political career, he had dismissed the idea that Americans of color deserved the same rights of citizenship that he enjoyed; these people were his social and political inferiors. He had articulated that view in public debates and in private writings and held that view even as he entered the White House. Through the first twenty months of the war, he had pushed for a colonization plan that would exile African Americans in a distant continent so that they would cause his nation no further consternation. He had once blamed black people for the nation's civil war. But in desperate need of men to fight his war, Lincoln had invited black men to join the Union army. After that—after African Americans demonstrated their mettle on the battlefield—he had begun to see them differently. They became his countrymen, fighting for his nation's cause. Lincoln had tolerated slavery, to a great extant, because he assumed the inferiority of black people. Now, however, having become aware of the black man's humanity during the crucible of combat, he simultaneously recognized slavery's inhumanity, and he criticized it in the harshest terms. In his Second Inaugural Address, Lincoln offered no specific agenda to extend to Americans of color the constitutional rights that he now undoubtedly realized they deserved. But he did speak of binding up the nation's wounds. As Phillip Shaw Paludan states, since Lincoln "had mentioned wounds drawn by the lash and by the sword, the wounds of slavery as well as of war needed care."[41] Lincoln hinted that, after the war, the nation would have to care for all of its inhabitants.

African Americans who heard the address understood perfectly what Lincoln was saying, and they sensed that the speech had a special meaning for them. The *New York Herald* reported that the "Negroes ejaculated 'bress de Lord' in a low murmur at the end of almost every sentence."[42] They realized that they were hearing a solemn and profound sermon, similar to the ones that they heard so often in their Baptist churches. When Frederick Douglass met Lincoln at an Inauguration Day reception at the White House, Douglass told the president that his address was "a sacred effort." Douglass later stated that Lincoln's Second Inaugural Address "sounded more like a sermon than like a state paper."[43] He, too, sensed that Lincoln was revealing a new way of thinking about slavery and the position of black Americans.

But not all of Lincoln's listeners understood or liked what they heard. As was the case with so much that Lincoln said and did, the reviews of the Second Inaugural Address were mixed. For the most part, pro-Republican newspapers praised the speech, while the newspapers that leaned toward the Democratic Party panned it. The *New York Herald* stated, "It was not strictly an inaugural address. . . . It was more like a valedictory."[44] Lincoln's home-state *Illinois Register* reported that the inaugural address was "not a very felicitous nor satisfactory performance." The *Chicago Tribune* called the address "strong in its naturalness and impressive in its simplicity, directness and force"; its rival newspaper, the *Chicago Times*, was less than flattering: "By the side of it, mediocrity is superb."[45] Charles F. Adams Jr., however, applauded the speech's "grand simplicity and directness" and deemed it "the historical keynote of the war."[46]

Twentieth-century commentators have been almost uniformly approving of Lincoln's Second Inaugural Address. Kazin calls it "the most remarkable inaugural address in our history—the only one that reflected literary genius."[47] Wolf regards the address as "a charter of Christian statesmanship."[48] Similarly, Elton Trueblood considers it "a theological classic."[49] Miller applauds Lincoln's speech for providing "a contrast, and perhaps a corrective, to the thread of national self-congratulation that is woven into American history."[50]

Lincoln's own words of evaluation are instructive. On March 15, 1865, Lincoln commented on his Second Inaugural Address in a letter to Thurlow Weed, a Republican Party supporter from New York:

> I expect the latter [the address] to wear as well as—perhaps better than—any thing I have produced; but I believe it is not immediately popular. Men are not flattered by being shown that there has been a difference of purpose between the Almighty and them. To deny it, however, in this case, is to deny that there is a God governing the world. It is a truth which I thought needed to be told; and as whatever of humiliation there is in it, falls most directly on myself, I thought others might afford for me to tell it. (8:356)

Besides claiming that his address would wear well, Lincoln here revealed that he had used the forum offered by the inauguration to make public his most deeply held conclusions about the key issues facing his nation. He had delivered to his nation a disturbing message that might not be immediately politically popular; he had not offered political "spin" to make his administration look good; he had not gloated about the North's impending victory in the war; nor had he offered a proposition that would be constantly tested, as he had offered at Gettysburg. Instead, he had conveyed "a truth . . . needed to be told."

Donald and Einhorn suggest that in the Second Inaugural Address, Lincoln absolves himself from any guilt over the war or slavery, that he shifts the responsibility for the conflict and its cause to God.[51] Lincoln's comments to Weed, however, refute Donald's and Einhorn's argument. Lincoln told Weed that "whatever of humiliation" there is in this truth that he told "falls most directly" on himself. In other words, if it is humiliating to learn that God's purpose differs from one's own, then Lincoln himself deserves the lion's share of humiliation. For a long time, he and his God had worked at cross purposes. God had desired to rid America of slavery, but Lincoln had been working to accommodate it; his whole political career had been crafted upon a so-called middle position on slavery: He would oppose it on moral grounds but tolerate it for political reasons; he would oppose its expansion to new territories but allow it to remain where it already existed. He won the White House by advancing this platform. When he faced the nation on March 4, 1865, he announced that he had been wrong, and now he felt the humiliation that results from two decades of erroneous thinking.

Guilt is often the residue of humiliation. Lincoln's fictional counterpart is Hawthorne's Dimmesdale, who delivers his election sermon in a voice scarred by anguish—the "complaint of a human heart, sorrow-laden, perchance guilty, telling its secret, whether of guilt or sorrow, to the great heart of mankind; beseeching its sympathy or forgiveness,—at every moment,—in each accent,—and never in vain!"[52] Like Lincoln, Dimmesdale had delivered a poignant message and, shortly thereafter, forever departed:

> His subject, it appeared, had been the relation between the Deity and the communities of mankind, with a special reference to the New En-

gland which they were here planting in the wilderness. And, as he drew towards the close, a spirit of prophecy had come upon him, constraining him to its purpose as mightily as the old prophets of Israel were constrained; only with this difference, that, whereas the Jewish seers had denounced judgments and ruin on their country, it was his mission to foretell a high and glorious destiny for the newly gathered people of the Lord. But throughout it all, and through the whole discourse, there had been a certain deep, sad undertone of pathos, which could not be interpreted otherwise than as the natural regret of one soon to pass away. . . . [T]heir minister . . . had the foreboding of untimely death upon him, and would soon leave them in tears![53]

In a sense, Lincoln, too, had forecast his own death. The blood drawn by the lash would be sunk with blood drawn by the sword. Lincoln, too, was guilty of allowing slavery to continue past God's appointed time. Lincoln's blood would have to be shed before slavery's debt was paid. Then the war would end. Lincoln had finally and firmly grasped the meaning of the war that consumed his nation, and he had communicated, in eloquent words on Inauguration Day, that meaning to his countrymen and countrywomen. He had told them a truth that he needed to reveal and that they needed to hear. But he would have only forty-one more days to act upon his newly revealed knowledge. As White suggests, the Second Inaugural Address is "Lincoln's last will and testament to the American nation."[54]

Epilogue

ON JULY 8, 1864, Abraham Lincoln, after deciding not to sign a stringent reconstruction bill passed by both houses of Congress, issued a Proclamation Concerning Reconstruction. Lincoln thought that the measure passed by Congress, which, among other demands, mandated that rebellious states desiring to rejoin the Union produce loyalty oaths signed by 50 percent of eligible voters, would dissuade Southern states from attempting to realign themselves with the Union. In his proclamation, Lincoln stated that he would not be "inflexibly committed to any single plan of restoration" (7:433). In Louisiana and Arkansas, reconstruction plans were already in place, and Lincoln did not want to sign legislation that would invalidate those efforts. Lincoln pledged his support for any rebellious state wishing to adopt the plan proposed by Congress, but he wanted the flexibility to evaluate other plans proposed by individual Southern states. He was a man open to any possibilities presented by the war's end. What he had said concerning reconstruction on December 15, 1863, still applied as the war came to a close: "I wish to avoid both the substance and the appearance of dictation" (7:67).

Where Lincoln was taking the nation in 1865 was not quite clear, even to himself. He had no historical precedents from which to work; the nation had never experienced secession or civil war. Lincoln would have to work out the details of reconstruction as he went along. David Herbert Donald reports that one of Lincoln's favorite mottos in office was "My policy is to have no policy," and this strategy certainly applied to reconstruction.[1] Although Lincoln had been considering the issues surrounding reconstruction since late April 1862, when Admiral David Farragut's fleet captured New Orleans and brought large areas of Louisiana under Union control, serious questions about reconstruction remained as Lincoln began his second term in office. Moreover, the North's victory in the war was not assured until General Robert E. Lee's surrender in April 1865; until that time, Lincoln was focused mainly on winning the war rather than on dealing with postwar issues. Hence, Lincoln's writings and speeches offer few specific reconstruction policies. Nonetheless, the general direction in which he was moving is fairly apparent.

Slavery was dead; the great national offense defined in the Second Inaugural Address was a casualty of the war. In every memorandum and statement about the South's readmission to the Union, Lincoln emphasized that acceptance of the Emancipation Proclamation and approval of the Thirteenth Amendment to the Constitution were requirements on which he could not compromise. "My enemies condemn my emancipation policy. Let them prove by the history of this war, that we can restore the Union without it," he told an interviewer in August 1864 (7:507). On April 5, 1865, Lincoln wrote to John A. Campbell, a Virginian, and spelled out the three major requirements for a rebellious state's readmission to the Union:

> As to peace, I have said before, and now repeat, that three things are indispensable:
> 1. The restoration of the national authority throughout all the States.
> 2. No receding by the Executive of the United States on the slavery question, from the position assumed thereon, in the late Annual Message to Congress, and in preceding documents.
> 3. No cessation of hostilities short of an end of the war, and the disbanding of all force hostile to the government. (8:386)

Lincoln was inflexible on those points, and he had made that known in several earlier statements.

But other civil rights issues remained unsettled as Lincoln began his second term in office and the war came to a close. What would become of the four million African Americans who had been made free during the war? Where would they work? What role would they play in postwar American society? Would they be granted any political, social, or legal rights that African Americans did not hold before the war? Lincoln had offered no statements about his thinking on these crucial issues in his Second Inaugural Address, but his last public address, a speech on reconstruction delivered on April 11, 1865, provided a few hints.

"We meet this evening, not in sorrow, but in gladness of heart," Lincoln began (8:399). Lee had surrendered his Army of Northern Virginia two days earlier, and Federal troops occupied Richmond and Petersburg. Union victories had given the nation "hope of a righteous and speedy peace whose joyous expression can not be restrained" (8:399). Lincoln quickly added a prayer of thanks: "He, from Whom all blessings flow, must not be forgotten. A call for a national thanksgiving is being prepared, and will be duly promulgated" (8:399–400). God had apparently deemed that the nation had paid its debt accumulated during 250 years of unrequited toil, and Lincoln was offering thanks. Lincoln also noted that the immediate future would prove challenging for the nation: "It is fraught with great difficulty. Unlike the case of a war between independent nations, there is no authorized organ for us to treat with" (8:400). Lincoln then repeated his desire for flexibility in bringing individual states back into proper alignment with the Union, that he was not committed to a single plan for reconstruction. He tactfully sidestepped the issue of whether the rebellious states had been in or out of the Union during the war:

> We all agree that the seceded States, so called, are out of their proper practical relation with the Union; and that the sole object of the government, civil and military, in regard to those States is to again get them into that proper practical relation. I believe it is not only possible, but in fact, easier, to do this, without deciding, or even considering, whether these states have even been out of the Union, than with it. Finding themselves safely at home, it would be utterly immaterial whether they had ever been abroad. (8:403)

To a great extent, Lincoln, in this address, was defending his policy for bringing Louisiana into proper practical relation with the Union.

He acknowledged that some of his critics would have preferred fifty, thirty, or even twenty thousand names on Louisiana's loyalty petition, rather than only twelve thousand names. Lincoln also conceded that many Northerners wanted to see Louisiana's new constitution guarantee "the elective franchise" to "the colored man" (8:403). The new constitution neither guaranteed nor prohibited voting rights for Louisiana's African American men; the constitution did allow the state legislature to grant voting rights in the future. On this point, Lincoln added, "I would myself prefer that it were now conferred on the very intelligent, and on those who serve our cause as soldiers" (8:403). Lincoln concluded the address by asserting that Louisiana's reconstruction plan was good both for white citizens, because it brought the state quickly back into the Union, and black citizens, because it formally abolished slavery.

By far, Lincoln's most important, and revealing, statement in this address was his personal comment concerning voting rights for "the colored man." He had, of course, made this point before in private letters to General James Wadsworth and to Michael Hahn, the free-state governor of Louisiana, but never in a public address. Phillip Shaw Paludan claims that Lincoln's address on reconstruction was "the first statement in the nation's history by a chief executive to endorse black voting."[2] Critics of Lincoln who argue that he never moved very far on civil rights issues point out that he desired to place restrictions on black voters that he would never force upon white voters—the elective franchise would be conferred only upon very intelligent black men and those who fought to save the Union. But perhaps Lincoln, sensing almost universal opposition in the South and widespread opposition in the North to voting rights for African Americans, was merely being prudent, initiating a one-step-at-a-time approach to reconstruction. Fawn M. Brodie suggests that Lincoln's limited suffrage "pointed the way to eventual universal Negro suffrage."[3] Stephen B. Oates concedes that Lincoln did not force African American suffrage on the South as a condition of readmission to the Union, but on the suffrage issue, Lincoln "displayed the same capacity for growth and change that had characterized his approach to emancipation."[4]

One man who heard Lincoln's address of April 11, 1865, sensed where Lincoln was going with his talk of voting rights for intelligent blacks and for those who served in the Union army. After Lincoln completed his speech, John Wilkes Booth, who had also attended Lincoln's Second Inaugural Address, reportedly grumbled to his companions, both Southern sympathizers, "That means nigger citizenship. Now, by God, I'll put him through. That is the last speech he will ever make."[5] Booth made good on his threat three days later.

Whether Booth was correct about Lincoln's direction on civil rights is not certain. Lincoln never made a statement concerning full citizenship rights for freed slaves and African American freemen. His most far-reaching statements on civil rights were generally limited to blacks who had fought in the Union army. During the war, he had come to realize the basic equality of all soldiers. Black and white soldiers deserved the same protection when they were captured and the same pay. The widows and orphans of all soldiers deserved equivalent government care and support in the form of pensions. Whenever Lincoln mentioned voting rights for African Americans, he stressed that black soldiers deserved first consideration. Almost two hundred thousand African American soldiers had served in the Union army and navy, and their performance in combat had forced him to cast aside some of the racial stereotypes that he had embraced before the war. Their stalwart service, according to Donald, "eroded his earlier doubts about their courage and intelligence."[6]

But would Lincoln, after the war, take the next step in the direction toward equal civil rights for all Americans? Or would only black war veterans enjoy some limited political rights while the rest of America's citizens of color languished in a state that offered little more than slavery? Some Lincoln scholars see little or no movement on Lincoln's part in the area of civil rights. Don E. Fehrenbacher maintains that, on civil rights issues, Lincoln "had none of the moral conviction that inspired his opposition to slavery. He never seems to have suspected that systematic racial discrimination might be, like slavery, a stain on the national honor and a crime against mankind."[7] Lerone Bennett Jr. states that Lincoln's reconstruction plans were "of the white people, by the white people, for the white people."[8]

Other Lincoln scholars, however, disagree and suggest that he saw the need for extending some basic rights of citizenship to the freed slaves. Paludan believes that Lincoln was shifting closer to members of Congress who espoused "expanded rights for blacks and . . . greater protection of those rights."[9] LaWanda Cox concurs. She sees in Lincoln's Louisiana reconstruction policy evidence that Lincoln was not prepared "in the interest of reunion and reconciliation to return political power to the antebellum landed elite" or "in the interest of either reunion or party to sacrifice the freedman." According to Cox, Lincoln and the Radical Republicans "shared an identity of purpose . . . in seeking basic rights, citizenship, and political participation for former slaves."[10] Oates maintains that in the area of civil rights for African Americans, Lincoln "was ahead of most members of his party—and far ahead of the vast majority of northern whites at the time."[11]

Unfortunately, Booth's bullet ended Lincoln's life before the president could fully flesh out his reconstruction plans on paper. We can only speculate about the direction in which he would go. It is not a stretch, however, to suggest that Lincoln was walking, one step at a time, down a road that it would take most of his countrymen and countrywomen one hundred years to find, that his recognition of the humanity of the African American soldier would be a gateway toward a fuller acknowledgment of the rights of all Americans, regardless of color. To push that point, a contemporary comparison might be useful. In 1947, Jackie Robinson integrated Major League Baseball. "As many ball players, officials, umpires and journalists envisioned it, the entity of baseball rose in alabaster, a temple of white supremacy," writes Roger Kahn in *The Boys of Summer*, his splendid study of Robinson's Brooklyn Dodgers. "To them, the Robinson presence was a defilement and the whites who consented to play at his side were whores." Robinson's teammates, however, came to admire him as a fierce competitor. "No one prattled about team spirit. No one made speeches on the Rights of Man. No one sang 'Let My People Go.' But without pretense or visible fear these men marched unevenly against the sin of bigotry," writes Kahn.[12]

According to Kahn, fans attending Robinson's home games at Ebbets Field soon got the message. They rooted for Robinson as they rooted for every other hometown player. "By applauding Robinson, a man did not feel that he was taking a stand on school integration, or on open housing," states Kahn. "But for an instant he had accepted Robinson simply as a hometown ball player. To disregard color, even for an instant, is to step away from the old prejudices, the old hatred. That is not a path on which many double back."[13]

Perhaps Lincoln had found that path; perhaps he was, in 1865, marching unevenly against the sin of bigotry. Perhaps in seeing the black soldier as a Union warrior, he had begun the process of casting aside color and race in his evaluation of human beings. If so, the man from racist Illinois was indeed stepping away from the old prejudices of his time and place. Lincoln had not double-backed on emancipation, despite great pressure to do so, and he would probably not have retreated on his commitment to voting rights for intelligent blacks and for African American war veterans. Perhaps the logic that he applied in so many other political situations would also have dictated that all blacks, not just the intelligentsia and those in the military, required the elective franchise if his nation were to experience fully the new birth of freedom that he spoke about at Gettysburg. Oates finds it obvious in which direction Lincoln was going on civil rights issues in 1865—"that was toward full political rights for the Negro, not away from them."[14]

Lincoln's treatment of individual citizens of color provides support for Oates's assertion. According to Richard N. Current, Lincoln "made the White House a scene of practical demonstrations of respect for human worth and dignity"; he "greeted Negro visitors as no President had done before."[15] Lincoln received African American visitors frequently, and he treated them with the utmost respect and courtesy. Frederick Douglass, who called upon Lincoln at the White House at least three times, noted that Lincoln very quickly put him at ease during his visits. Douglass, who often strongly criticized Lincoln for moving too slowly on emancipation and on civil rights issues, nonetheless claimed that Lincoln was completely free from racial prejudice. "In his company," wrote Douglass, "I was never in any way reminded of my humble origin, or my unpopular color."[16] And Douglass was not the only black person to make that point. Sojourner Truth, a former slave and an abolitionist and women's rights orator, commented that she "never was treated by any one with more kindness and cordiality" than that shown by Lincoln when she visited the White House.[17] Similarly, Elizabeth Keckley, Mary Todd Lincoln's seamstress and confidant, testified in her autobiography to the respect that Lincoln always demonstrated in her presence. "[H]e always called me Madam Elizabeth," she stated at one point in her narrative.[18]

Sad are the times when a white man is applauded for showing people of color the common courtesies due any human being. But such manners as those displayed by Lincoln in the presence of African American visitors were hardly the norm in the 1860s. By contrast, consider Douglass's visit to the White House during the days of Andrew Johnson's administration. Douglass, with other African American civil rights leaders, was calling upon Johnson to voice their protest against his opposition to voting rights for black citizens of Washington, D.C. Johnson quickly dismissed his petitioners; after they departed, he said to his secretary, "Those damned sons of bitches thought they had me in a trap. I know that damned Douglass; he's just like any other nigger, and he would sooner cut a white man's throat than not."[19]

Lincoln surely would not have approached reconstruction as Johnson did. During his presidency and the war, Lincoln had demonstrated a remarkable capacity for growth, particularly in the area of civil rights. The reluctant abolitionist became, by the time of his Second Inaugural Address, the secular minister who scolded his community for the sin of slavery. The man who reasoned that black soldiers would quickly surrender their arms in battle became the man who argued that the recruitment of African American troops turned the tide of the Civil War. The man who once proposed to exile black Americans to other continents became the man who spoke of voting rights for at least some African American citizens. He had experienced religious growth, too, during his White House years. The political candidate once derided as an infidel became a president who tried to square the nation's commitments to what he perceived as God's plan. Wendell Phillips, an abolitionist and civil rights advocate who was often impatient with Lincoln, once stated that Lincoln was able to grow only because "we have watered him."[20] That might be partially true, but other American presidents, too, were watered and did not grow as Lincoln did.

Lincoln, during the last two years of his life, had begun, with his words and his policies, to outgrow the prejudices of his time and place. Allen C. Guelzo suggests that he had begun to redefine the concept of nationhood, that "he made the idea of the nation—a single people unified rationally . . . around certain propositions that transcended ethnicity, religious denominationalism, and gender—into the central image of the republic."[21] Booth's bullet deprived the nation of the benefits of his growth at a time of great national strife. Without Lincoln, the nation remained a racially divided house for at least another century; Reconstruction actually lasted through the 1960s. Writing during that racially troubled decade, Reinhold Niebuhr stated, "The stubbornness of the South's resistance to the integration movement is part of the price we pay for the vindictiveness which Lincoln would have avoided."[22] Lincoln's abrupt death in 1865, just more than a month after he revealed to his fellow Americans a truth needed to be told for then and for all time, was the nation's greatest tragedy, one from which it has never truly recovered.

APPENDIX

The Second Inaugural Address

FELLOW COUNTRYMEN:

At this second appearing to take the oath of the presidential office, there is less occasion for an extended address than there was at the first. Then a statement, somewhat in detail, of a course to be pursued, seemed fitting and proper. Now, at the expiration of four years, during which public declarations have been constantly called forth on every point and phase of the great contest which still absorbs the attention, and engrosses the energies of the nation, little that is new could be presented. The progress of our arms, upon which all else chiefly depends, is as well known to the public as to myself; and it is, I trust, reasonably satisfactory and encouraging to all. With high hopes for the future, no prediction in regard to it is ventured.

On the occasion corresponding to this four years ago, all thoughts were anxiously directed to an impending civil-war. All dreaded it—all sought to avert it. While the inaugural address was being delivered from this place, devoted altogether to *saving* the Union without war, insurgent agents were in the city seeking to *destroy* it without war—seeking to dissolve the Union, and divide its effects, by negotiation. Both parties deprecated war; but one of them would *make* war rather than let the nation survive; and the other would *accept* war rather than let it perish. And the war came.

One eighth of the whole population were colored slaves, not distributed generally over the Union, but localized in the Southern part of it. These slaves constituted a peculiar and powerful interest. All knew that this interest was, somehow, the cause of the war. To strengthen, perpetuate, and extend this interest was the object for which the insurgents would rend the Union, even by war; while the government claimed no right to do more than to restrict the territorial enlargement of it. Neither party expected for the war, the magnitude, or the duration, which it has already attained. Neither anticipated that the *cause* of the conflict might cease with, or even before, the conflict itself should cease. Each looked for an easier triumph, and a result less fundamental and astounding. Both read the same Bible, and pray to the same God; and each invokes His aid against the other. It may seem strange that any men should dare ask a just God's assistance in wringing their bread from the sweat of other men's faces; but let us judge not that we be not judged. The prayers of both could not be answered; that of neither has been answered fully. The Almighty has His own purposes. "Woe unto the world because of offences! for it must needs be that offences come; but woe to that man by whom the offence cometh!" If we shall suppose that American Slavery is one of those offences which, in the providence of God, must needs come, but which, having continued through His appointed time, He now wills to remove, and that He gives to both North and South, this terrible war as the woe due to those by whom the offence came, shall we discern therein any departure from those divine attributes which the believers in a Living God always ascribe to Him? Fondly do we hope—fervently do we pray—that this mighty scourge of war may speedily pass away. Yet, if God wills that it continue, until all the wealth piled by the bond-man's two hundred and fifty years of unrequited toil shall be sunk, and until every drop of blood drawn with the lash, shall be paid by another drawn with the sword, as was said three thousand years ago, so still it must be said "the judgments of the Lord, are true and righteous altogether."

With malice toward none; with charity for all; with firmness in the right, as God gives us to see the right, let us strive on to finish the work we are in; to bind up the nation's wounds; to care for him who shall have borne the battle, and for his widow, and his orphan—to do all which may achieve and cherish a just, and a lasting peace, among ourselves, and with all nations.

NOTES

INTRODUCTION

1. Thomas Geoghegan, "Lincoln Apologizes," *New York Times*, April 5, 1998. Wills's book is titled *Lincoln at Gettysburg: The Words That Remade America* (New York: Simon & Schuster, 1992). Wills, perhaps, did respond to Geoghegan's call by publishing a lengthy article on Lincoln's Second Inaugural Address titled "Lincoln's Greatest Speech?" in the September 1999 issue of *Atlantic Monthly*, but he has yet to expand his ideas on the Second Inaugural into a book. Early in 2002, while this present text was in the process of publication, Ronald C. White Jr. published *Lincoln's Greatest Speech: The Second Inaugural* (New York: Simon & Schuster, 2002).

2. Besides Wills's text, see also Allan Nevins, ed., *Lincoln and the Gettysburg Address: Commemorative Papers* (Urbana: University of Illinois Press, 1964); Philip B. Kunhardt, *A New Birth of Freedom: Lincoln at Gettysburg* (Boston: Little, Brown, 1983); Louis A. Warren, *Lincoln's Gettysburg Declaration: "A New Birth of Freedom"* (Fort Wayne, Ind.: Lincoln National Life Foundation, 1964); and William Eleazar, *Lincoln and Gettysburg: What He Intended to Say; What He Said; What He Was Reported to Have Said; What He Wished He Had Said* (New York: P. Smith, 1930).

3. Wills, *Lincoln at Gettysburg*, 189.

4. William Lee Miller, "Lincoln's Second Inaugural: The Zenith of Statecraft," *Center Magazine*, July/August 1980, 53.

5. In Plato's *Apology*, Socrates, on trial for his life, informs the court that "the life which is unexamined is not worth living." See Christopher Biffle, *A Guided Tour of Five Works by Plato*, 3rd ed. (Mountain View, Calif.: Mayfield Publishing, 2001), 47.

6. Edgar Lee Masters, *Lincoln the Man* (New York: Dodd, Mead, 1931).

7. Carl Sandburg, *Abraham Lincoln: The Prairie Years*, 2 vols. (New York: Harcourt, Brace & World, 1926). Four subsequent volumes under the title of *Abraham Lincoln: The War Years* appeared in 1939.

8. Edmund Wilson, *Patriotic Gore: Studies in the Literature of the American Civil War* (New York: Oxford University Press, 1962), 115, xviii–xix, xxxi.

9. Alfred Kazin, *God and the American Writer* (New York: Vintage Books, 1997), 140.

10. William J. Wolf, *Lincoln's Religion* (Philadelphia: Pilgrim Press, 1970), 24. This text appeared earlier under the titles *The Almost Chosen People* and *The Religion of Abraham Lincoln*.

11. John Dos Passos, "Lincoln and His Almost Chosen People," in Nevins, *Lincoln and the Gettysburg Address*, 33.

12. Allen C. Guelzo, *Abraham Lincoln: Redeemer President* (Grand Rapids, Mich.: William B. Eerdmans, 1999), 462.

13. Elton Trueblood, *Abraham Lincoln: Theologian of American Anguish* (New York: Harper & Row, 1973), 94.

14. Reinhold Niebuhr, "The Religion of Abraham Lincoln," in Nevins, *Lincoln and the Gettysburg Address*, 83.

15. Roy P. Basler, ed., *The Collected Works of Abraham Lincoln* (New Brunswick, N.J.: Rutgers University Press, 1953), 7:282. Future references to this eight-volume work appear parenthetically. I have taken the liberty of correcting the occasional spelling or capitalization error attributed to Lincoln.

16. Richard Hofstadter, *The American Political Tradition* (New York: Vintage Books, 1948), 95, 107–8.

17. Don E. Fehrenbacher, *Prelude to Greatness: Lincoln in the 1850s* (Stanford, Calif.: Stanford University Press, 1962), 23.

18. Guelzo, *Abraham Lincoln*, 182.

19. Joan D. Hedrick, *Harriet Beecher Stowe: A Life* (New York: Oxford University Press, 1994), 208.

20. Henry David Thoreau, *Civil Disobedience and Other Essays* (New York: Dover Publications, 1993), 23, 29.

21. Fehrenbacher, *Prelude to Greatness*, 22.

22. Lerone Bennett Jr., "Was Abe Lincoln a White Supremacist?" *Ebony*, February 1968, 35. Bennett expanded his critique of Lincoln into a book-length study in 2000: *Forced into Glory: Abraham Lincoln's White Dream* (Chicago: Johnson Publishing, 2000).

23. Julius Lester, *Look Out Whitey! Black Power's Gon' Get Your Mama!* (New York: Dial Press, 1968), 58.

24. Julie Salamon, "The Web as Home for Racism and Hate," *New York Times*, October 23, 2000.

25. Trueblood, *Abraham Lincoln*, viii.

26. James M. McPherson, "Lincoln the Devil," review of *Forced into Glory: Abraham Lincoln's White Dream*, by Lerone Bennett Jr., *New York Times Book Review*, August 27, 2000, 12.

27. Benjamin Quarles, *Lincoln and the Negro* (New York: Oxford University Press, 1962), preface, 13.

28. Fawn M. Brodie, "Who Defends the Abolitionist?" in *The Antislavery Vanguard: New Essays on the Abolitionists*, ed. Martin Duberman (Princeton, N.J.: Princeton University Press, 1965), 63–64.

29. Quarles, *Lincoln and the Negro*, 153.

30. David Herbert Donald, *Lincoln* (New York: Simon & Schuster, 1995), 14.

31. Richard N. Current, *The Lincoln Nobody Knows* (New York: McGraw Hill, 1958), 235–36.

32. Stephen B. Oates, *Abraham Lincoln: The Man Behind the Myths* (New York: Harper & Row, 1984), 144.

33. LaWanda Cox, *Lincoln and Black Freedom: A Study of Presidential Leadership* (Columbia: University of South Carolina Press, 1981), 6.

34. Mark E. Neely Jr., *The Last Best Hope of Earth: Abraham Lincoln and the Promise of America* (Cambridge: Harvard University Press, 1993), vii.

35. Don E. Fehrenbacher, *Lincoln in Text and Context* (Stanford, Calif.: Stanford University Press, 1987), 96.

36. A vast number of biographies of Lincoln and histories of his era already exist. Excellent single-volume biographies of Lincoln include Stephen B. Oates, *With Malice Toward None: The Life of Abraham Lincoln* (New York: Harper & Row, 1977); and Donald, *Lincoln*. A superb history of Lincoln's era is James M. McPherson, *Battle Cry of Freedom: The Civil War Era* (New York: Oxford University Press, 1988).

37. Unlike contemporary presidents who employ a team of speechwriters, Lincoln generally crafted his own speeches.

38. Current, *Lincoln Nobody Knows*, 17.

39. William H. Herndon and Jesse William Weik, *Herndon's Lincoln: The True Story of a Great Life* (Springfield, Ill.: Herndon's Lincoln Publishing Co., 1889).

40. Michael Burlingame, *The Inner World of Abraham Lincoln* (Urbana and Chicago: University of Illinois Press, 1994), xxiv.

41. Douglas L. Wilson, *Honor's Voice: The Transformation of Abraham Lincoln* (New York: Alfred A. Knopf, 1998), 11.

42. Charles B. Strozier, *Lincoln's Quest for Union: Public and Private Meanings* (New York: Basic Books, 1982), xiv–xv.

43. Benjamin Barondess, *Three Lincoln Masterpieces: Cooper Institute Speech, Gettysburg Address, Second Inaugural* (Charleston: Education Foundation of West Virginia, 1954), 43–44.

44. Louis A. Warren, *Lincoln's Gettysburg Declaration: "A New Birth of Freedom"* (Fort Wayne, Ind.: Lincoln National Life Foundation, 1964), 126.

45. Wills, *Lincoln at Gettysburg*, 36.

46. Roy P. Basler, foreword to *Collected Works of Abraham Lincoln*, 1:xv.

47. Donald, *Lincoln*, 566.

48. Ibid., 566–68; Neely, *Last Best Hope*, 156.

CHAPTER ONE

1. Hofstadter, *American Political Tradition*, 109.

2. George M. Fredrickson, ed., *William Lloyd Garrison* (Englewood Cliffs, N.J.: Prentice-Hall, 1968), 23.

3. Bennett, "Was Abe Lincoln a White Supremacist?" 36.

4. Hofstadter, *American Political Tradition*, 97.

5. Neely, *Last Best Hope*, 24.

6. Burlingame, *Inner World of Abraham Lincoln*, 37; Guelzo, *Abraham Lincoln*, 121.

7. Wilson, *Honor's Voice*, 166.

8. Herbert Mitgang, "Was Lincoln Just a Honki?" *New York Times Magazine*, February 11, 1968, 100.

9. Donald, *Lincoln*, 104.

10. Quarles, *Lincoln and the Negro*, 25.

11. John Woolman, *The Journal and Other Writings of John Woolman* (New York: E. P. Dutton, 1922), 40.

12. Hofstadter, *American Political Tradition*, 110.

13. Guelzo, *Abraham Lincoln*, 140.

14. In a sense, the furor was over nothing. The Kansas-Nebraska Act was largely symbolic, as slavery would take hold in neither Kansas nor Nebraska. The 1860 census showed fifteen slaves in Nebraska and two in Kansas. See Current, *Lincoln Nobody Knows*, 95.

15. Quarles, *Lincoln and the Negro*, 33.

16. Waldo Braden, *Abraham Lincoln: Public Speaker* (Baton Rouge: Louisiana State University Press, 1988), 35–36.

17. Neely, *Last Best Hope*, 39.

18. Lincoln's secretaries, John Nicolay and John Hay, assign a date of July 1, 1854, to this fragment, but Roy P. Basler suggests that it probably belongs to a later period (*Collected Works*, 2:223n). Lincoln might have been considering using this fragment in a speech, or he might have been working out an idea on paper, as he sometimes did.

19. *Dred Scott v. John F. A. Sandford*, 19 Howard 393, in *The Dred Scott Decision: Law or Politics*, ed. Stanley I. Kutler (Boston: Houghton Mifflin, 1967), 24.

20. Guelzo, *Abraham Lincoln*, 196.

21. David Zarefsky, *Lincoln, Douglas and Slavery: In the Crucible of Public Debate* (Chicago: University of Chicago Press, 1990), 85–86. The *Lemmon* case was made moot by the secession crisis of 1861.

22. Fehrenbacher, *Prelude to Greatness*, 94.

23. Hofstadter, *American Political Tradition*, 116.

24. Zarefsky, *Lincoln, Douglas and Slavery*, 35.

25. Ibid., 25.

26. Ibid., 166.

27. Ibid., 276.

28. According to Basler, this speech was never actually delivered (*Collected Works*, 4:201n).

29. Don E. Fehrenbacher, "Lincoln and the Constitution," in *The Public and Private Lincoln: Contemporary Perspectives*, ed. Cullom Davis, Charles B. Strozier, Rebecca Monroe Veach, and Geoffrey C. Ward (Carbondale: Southern Illinois University Press, 1979), 134.

30. Phillip Shaw Paludan, *The Presidency of Abraham Lincoln* (Lawrence: University Press of Kansas, 1994), 56. Similarly, Lois J. Einhorn states that Lincoln's First Inaugural "was a conservative document that defended the status quo. . . . [H]e admitted that the status quo was not perfect but argued that it was as good as it could be." See *Abraham Lincoln the Orator* (Westport, Conn.: Greenwood Press, 1992), 62.

31. Paludan, *Presidency of Abraham Lincoln*, 56.

32. Zarefsky, *Lincoln, Douglas and Slavery*, 184.

33. Niebuhr, "Religion of Abraham Lincoln," 83.

34. Martin Duberman, "The Northern Response to Slavery," in *The Antislavery Vanguard*, ed. Martin Duberman (Princeton, N.J.: Princeton University Press, 1965), 402.

35. Paludan, *Presidency of Abraham Lincoln*, 16.

CHAPTER TWO

1. Neely, *Last Best Hope*, 42.

2. Stephen B. Oates, *Our Fiery Trial: Abraham Lincoln, John Brown, and the Civil War* (Amherst: University of Massachusetts Press, 1979), 66.

3. Zarefsky, *Lincoln, Douglas and Slavery*, 27.

4. Wills, *Lincoln at Gettysburg*, 92.

5. Leon F. Litwack, *North of Slavery: The Negro in the Free States 1790–1860* (Chicago: University of Chicago Press, 1961), vii.

6. Fehrenbacher, *Lincoln in Text and Context*, 106–7.

7. Hofstadter, *American Political Tradition*, 117n.

8. Neely, *Last Best Hope*, 41; Bennett, "Was Abe Lincoln a White Supremacist?" 36.

9. Niebuhr, "Religion of Abraham Lincoln," 81–82.

10. Zarefsky, *Lincoln, Douglas and Slavery*, 35.

11. George Fitzhugh articulates this view in his 1857 book, *Cannibals All! Or, Slaves Without Masters*, ed. C. Van Woodward (Cambridge: Harvard University Press, 1960), 31.

12. Zarefsky, *Lincoln, Douglas and Slavery*, 183.

13. Cox, *Lincoln and Black Freedom*, 22.

14. Fehrenbacher, *Prelude to Greatness*, 111.

15. Oates, *Abraham Lincoln*, 72.

16. Paludan, *Presidency of Abraham Lincoln*, 19.

17. Zarefsky, *Lincoln, Douglas and Slavery*, 79.

18. Quarles, *Lincoln and the Negro*, 36.

19. Donald, *Lincoln*, 221.

20. Strozier, *Lincoln's Quest*, 174.

21. Oates, *Abraham Lincoln*, 75.

22. Eric Foner, letter to the editor, *New York Times*, August 25, 2001.

23. Donald points out that Lincoln's famous line in the Gettysburg Address endorsing a government "of the people, by the people, for the people" was adapted from a speech by Theodore Parker. See Donald, *Lincoln*, 461.

24. Oates, *Abraham Lincoln*, 63.

25. John Rock articulated the position of many African Americans on colonization when he wrote in the *Liberator* early in 1860, "This being our country, we have made up our minds to remain in it, and try to make it worth living." See James M. McPherson, *The Negro's Civil War* (New York: Pantheon Books, 1965), 81. Chapter 6 of McPherson's book, "The Colonization Issue," presents a variety of opinions on the colonization issue.

26. Harriet Beecher Stowe, *Uncle Tom's Cabin* (1852; reprint, New York: Bantam Books, 1981), 443.

27. Paludan, *Presidency of Abraham Lincoln*, 107.

28. Neely, *Last Best Hope*, 43. Neely points out that Lincoln addressed the American Colonization Society in 1853 and 1855, but those speeches have not survived. According to Neely, "The accident of their failure to survive has probably helped Lincoln's reputation in modern times." See ibid.

29. Donald, *Lincoln*, 167.

30. Paludan, *Presidency of Abraham Lincoln*, 132.

31. Bennett, "Was Abe Lincoln a White Supremacist?" 38.

32. Strozier, *Lincoln's Quest*, 154.

33. Ibid.

34. According to John H. Wallace, "Black people have never accepted 'nigger' as a proper term—not in George Washington's time, Mark Twain's time, or William Faulkner's time." See "The Case Against *Huck Finn*," in *Satire or Evasion: Black Perspectives on* Huckleberry Finn, ed. James S. Leonard, Thomas A. Tenney, and Thadious M. Davis (Durham, N.C.: Duke University Press, 1992), 17.

35. Quarles, *Lincoln and the Negro*, 65.

CHAPTER THREE

1. Guelzo, *Abraham Lincoln*, 117.

2. Wolf, *Lincoln's Religion*, 72.

3. Anne Bradstreet, "To My Dear Children," in *The Puritans in America: A Narrative Anthology*, ed. Alan Heimert and Andrew Delbanco (Cambridge: Harvard University Press, 1985), 138.

4. Mary Rowlandson, *The Narrative of the Captivity and Restoration of Mrs. Mary Rowlandson* (1682; reprint, Lancaster, Mass.: Lancaster Bicentennial Commission, 1975), 51.

5. Jonathan Edwards, "Sinners in the Hands of an Angry God," in *Jonathan Edwards: Representative Selections*, ed. Clarence H. Faust and Thomas H. Johnson (New York: Hill and Wang, 1962), 163–64.

6. Wilson, *Patriotic Gore*, 91.

7. David Walker, "Walker's Appeal," in *The American Reader: Words That Moved a Nation*, ed. Diane Ravitch (New York: HarperCollins, 1990), 100.

8. Stowe, *Uncle Tom's Cabin*, 446.

9. Warren, *Lincoln's Gettysburg Declaration*, 11.

10. Wilson, *Patriotic Gore*, 114–15.

11. Wolf, *Lincoln's Religion*, 90.

12. Ibid., 42.

13. Wilson, *Honor's Voice*, 77–78.

14. Ibid., 187.

15. Wolf, *Lincoln's Religion*, 40, 48.

16. Trueblood, *Abraham Lincoln*, 97.

17. Wilson, *Honor's Voice*, 76.

18. Ibid., 259.

19. Donald, *Lincoln*, 15.

20. Wolf, *Lincoln's Religion*, 77.

21. Ibid., 78.

22. Niebuhr, "Religion of Abraham Lincoln," 75.

23. John Winthrop, "A Model of Christian Charity," in Heimert and Delbanco, *Puritans in America*, 89.

24. Winthrop, "Model of Christian Charity," 91. Peter Bulkeley, in "The Gospel-Covenant," written in 1639 or 1640, would repeat Winthrop's image of the city upon a hill: "And for ourselves here, the people of New England, we should in a special manner labor to shine forth in holiness above other people; we have that plenty and abundance of ordinances and means of grace, as few people enjoy the like. We are as a city set upon an hill, in the open view of all the earth; the eyes of the world are upon us because we profess ourselves to be a people in covenant with God." See Bulkeley, "The Gospel-Covenant," in Heimert and Delbanco, *Puritans in America*, 120.

25. Wilson, *Patriotic Gore*, 103.

26. Kazin, *God and the American Writer*, 139.

27. Wolf, *Lincoln's Religion*, 9.

CHAPTER FOUR

1. Fehrenbacher, "Lincoln and the Constitution," 134.

2. Donald, *Lincoln*, 305.

3. James M. McPherson, *Abraham Lincoln and the Second American Revolution* (New York: Oxford University Press, 1990), 128.

4. Bennett, "Was Abe Lincoln a White Supremacist?" 38.

5. Cox, *Lincoln and Black Freedom*, 10.

6. Neely, *Last Best Hope*, 101.

7. Donald, *Lincoln*, 368.

8. Fehrenbacher, *Lincoln in Text and Context*, 109.

9. Hofstadter, *American Political Tradition*, 131.

10. McPherson, *Negro's Civil War*, 162.

11. Lincoln's Central American colonization plan never came to fruition. A government-sponsored colonization plan in Haiti in 1863 and 1864 proved disastrous. See Quarles, *Lincoln and the Negro*, 192.

12. David W. Blight, *Frederick Douglass' Civil War: Keeping Faith in Jubilee* (Baton Rouge: Louisiana State University Press, 1989), 139.

13. Fehrenbacher, *Lincoln in Text and Context*, 111.

14. Paludan, *Presidency of Abraham Lincoln*, 151.

15. Neely, *Last Best Hope*, 110–11.

16. Ibid., 113.

17. Quarles, *Lincoln and the Negro*, 133.

18. Lincoln left no written comment on this matter. For a discussion of it, see Wolf, *Lincoln's Religion*, 17; Donald, *Lincoln*, 374; Guelzo, *Abraham Lincoln*, 341; and Trueblood, *Abraham Lincoln*, 45.

19. Current, *Lincoln Nobody Knows*, 62.

20. Wilson, *Patriotic Gore*, 104.

21. Trueblood, *Abraham Lincoln*, 8.

22. Guelzo, *Abraham Lincoln*, 327.

23. Wolf, *Lincoln's Religion*, 119.

24. Barbara J. Fields, "Who Freed the Slaves?" in *The Civil War: An Illustrated History*, by Geoffrey C. Ward, Ric Burns, and Ken Burns (New York: Alfred A. Knopf, 1990), 181.

CHAPTER FIVE

1. Karl Marx, "An Evaluation of Lincoln," in *Europe Looks at the Civil War*, ed. Bell Becker and Lillian Friedman (New York: Orion Press, 1960), 190–91.

2. Bennett, "Was Abe Lincoln a White Supremacist?" 40.

3. Donald, *Lincoln*, 375.

4. Quarles, *Lincoln and the Negro*, 149.

5. Neely, *Last Best Hope*, 115.

6. Hofstadter, *American Political Tradition*, 132.

7. Wills, *Lincoln at Gettysburg*, 142.

8. Martin Luther King Jr., *I Have a Dream: Writings and Speeches That Changed the World*, ed. James M. Washington (San Francisco: HarperSanFrancisco, 1992), 195.

9. Current, *Lincoln Nobody Knows,* 228.

10. Neely, *Last Best Hope,* 116.

11. Paludan, *Presidency of Abraham Lincoln,* 188.

12. Fields, "Who Freed the Slaves?" 181.

13. Current, *Lincoln Nobody Knows,* 227.

14. Oates, *Our Fiery Trial,* 77; Paludan, *Presidency of Abraham Lincoln,* 155.

15. George Anastaplo, *Abraham Lincoln: A Constitutional Biography* (Lanham, Md.: Rowman & Littlefield, 1999), 223.

16. Oates, *Abraham Lincoln,* 112. James M. McPherson and George Anastaplo make the same point. See McPherson, *Abraham Lincoln and the Second American Revolution,* 130; and Anastaplo, *Abraham Lincoln,* 224.

17. McPherson, *Abraham Lincoln and the Second American Revolution,* 85.

18. Quarles, *Lincoln and the Negro,* 150

19. Guelzo, *Abraham Lincoln,* 347.

20. See ibid., 371; Wills, *Lincoln at Gettysburg,* 103–6; and Glen E. Thurow, *Abraham Lincoln and American Political Religion* (Albany: State University of New York Press, 1976), 76.

21. Donald, *Lincoln,* 466.

22. McPherson, *Battle Cry of Freedom,* 594–95.

23. Hofstadter, *American Political Tradition,* 133.

24. Oates, *Abraham Lincoln,* 113.

25. Paludan, *Presidency of Abraham Lincoln,* 190.

26. McPherson, *Negro's Civil War,* 166.

27. Ibid., 168.

28. Ibid., 185.

29. Ibid., 187.

30. Ward, Burns, and Burns, *Civil War,* 248.

31. Quarles states that Lincoln's order "had a marked effect in protecting the great majority of captured Negro soldiers. . . . [I]n general, after Lincoln's order of retaliation, the Confederate authorities treated them much the same as they treated white prisoners." See Quarles, *Lincoln and the Negro,* 175. At Fort Pillow, Tennessee, in April 1864, however, Confederate soldiers under General Nathan Bedford Forrest executed white and black Union prisoners. Executions also occurred elsewhere after Lincoln's Order of Retaliation was issued. Lincoln's cabinet debated a response to Fort Pillow, but Lincoln, fearing an endless series of retaliations against innocent prisoners, ordered no execu-

tions of Confederate prisoners, a decision that Frederick Douglass and others protested. For a concise discussion, see McPherson, *Battle Cry of Freedom*, 793–95. For a more detailed discussion, see Richard L. Fuchs, *An Unerring Fire: The Massacre at Fort Pillow* (Rutherford, Madison, and Teaneck, N.J.: Fairleigh Dickinson University Press, 1994).

32. Paludan, *Presidency of Abraham Lincoln*, 300.

33. John Y. Simon, ed., *The Papers of Ulysses S. Grant*, vol. 9 (Carbondale and Edwardsville: Southern Illinois University Press, 1982), 196.

34. Ibid., 196–97.

35. Fehrenbacher, *Lincoln in Text and Context*, 275.

36. See Basler's footnote after the letter for an explanation (*Collected Works of Abraham Lincoln*, 7:102).

37. Cox, *Lincoln and Black Freedom*, 77.

38. Oates, *Abraham Lincoln*, 113.

39. This letter in not included in *The Collected Works of Abraham Lincoln* but is included in the supplement published twenty-one years later. My source is *Abraham Lincoln: Selected Speeches and Writings*, ed. Don E. Fehrenbacher (New York: Vintage Books/Library of America, 1992), 424.

40. For a detailed discussion of Mrs. Booth's appeal and the consequent congressional actions, see Roy P. Basler, "And for His Widow and His Orphan," *Quarterly Journal of the Library of Congress* 27 (October 1970): 291–94.

41. Basler, "And for His Widow," 294.

42. David Herbert Donald reports that Lincoln, in August 1864, briefly considered dropping the demand for the abolition of slavery as a condition for the South's return to the Union, but Frederick Douglass dissuaded Lincoln from taking this position. See Donald, *Lincoln*, 526–27.

43. By declaring national fast days, Lincoln was continuing a Puritan tradition. In colonial New England, during times of crisis, the governor or the General Court often would order days of fast and prayer. See Babette May Levy, *Preaching in the First Half Century of New England History* (New York: Russell & Russell, 1967), 86.

44. Trueblood, *Abraham Lincoln*, 32.

45. Niebuhr, "Religion of Abraham Lincoln," 75.

46. Oates, *Abraham Lincoln*, 118.

47. Fields, "Who Freed the Slaves?" 178.

CHAPTER SIX

1. Nathaniel Hawthorne, *The Scarlet Letter* (1850; reprint, New York: W. W. Norton, 1961), 161, 162–63, 170–71.

2. Sacvan Bercovitch, *The American Jeremiad* (Madison: University of Wisconsin Press, 1978), xi.

3. Ibid., 61.

4. Thomas Hooker, "The Application of Redemption," in Heimert and Delbanco, *Puritans in America*, 178.

5. Harry S. Stout, *The New England Soul: Preaching and Religious Culture in Colonial New England* (New York: Oxford University Press, 1986), 71.

6. A. W. Plumstead, *The Wall and the Garden: Selected Massachusetts Election Sermons 1670–1775* (Minneapolis: University of Minnesota Press, 1968), 16, 18.

7. Ibid., 3.

8. Garry Wills, "Lincoln's Greatest Speech?" *Atlantic Monthly*, September 1999, 62.

9. *Inaugural Addresses of the Presidents of the United States from George Washington 1789 to Richard Milhous Nixon 1969* (Washington, D.C.: Government Printing Office, 1969), 56.

10. See Wills, *Lincoln at Gettysburg*, 41–62.

11. See, for example, Wolf, *Lincoln's Religion*, 38; and Strozier, *Lincoln's Quest for Union*, 227.

12. Wilson, *Patriotic Gore*, 103.

13. Kazin, *God and the American Writer*, 134.

14. Barondess, *Three Lincoln Masterpieces*, 66.

15. Wills, "Lincoln's Greatest Speech?" 65.

16. Ibid., 68.

17. Barondess, *Three Lincoln Masterpieces*, 66.

18. Ronald C. White Jr. "Lincoln's Sermon on the Mount: The Second Inaugural" in *Religion and the American Civil War*, ed. Randall M. Miller, Harry S. Stout, and Charles Reagan Wilson (New York: Oxford University Press, 1998), 213.

19. Miller, "Lincoln's Second Inaugural," 55.

20. Einhorn, *Abraham Lincoln the Orator*, 87.

21. Oates, *Abraham Lincoln*, 118.

22. Wills, *Lincoln at Gettysburg*, 186.

23. Philip S. Foner, ed., *The Basic Writings of Thomas Jefferson* (Garden City, N.Y.: Halcyon House, 1950), 24.

24. Wilson, *Patriotic Gore*, 104–5.

25. Wills, *Lincoln at Gettysburg*, 184; Miller, "Lincoln's Second Inaugural," 56.

26. Kazin, *God and the American Writer*, 137, 129.

27. Braden, *Abraham Lincoln*, 95.

28. Guelzo, *Abraham Lincoln*, 417.

29. Donald, *Lincoln*, 567. Fehrenbacher makes a similar point about Lincoln's passage concerning the slave owner's lash and the soldier's sword: "Here was a cruel doctrine, offered to explain a cruel war. Yet the argument provided a logical basis for the principle of 'malice toward none,' because it absolved the South as well as the North from ultimate responsibility." See Fehrenbacher, *Lincoln in Text and Context*, 162–63. Lois J. Einhorn states that Lincoln assigned responsibility for slavery and the war to God. See Einhorn, *Abraham Lincoln the Orator*, 90.

30. Wills, "Lincoln's Greatest Speech?" 69.

31. Miller, "Lincoln's Second Inaugural," 60.

32. George M. Fredrickson, "The Search for Order and Community," in Davis et al., *Public and Private Lincoln*, 97.

33. Guelzo, *Abraham Lincoln*, 419.

34. McPherson, *American Lincoln and the Second American Revolution*, 36.

35. Wills, *Lincoln at Gettysburg*, 188.

36. Bercovitch, *American Jeremiad*, 8.

37. Wills, *Lincoln at Gettysburg*, 177.

38. Ibid., 37.

39. Donald, *Lincoln*, 566; Einhorn, *Abraham Lincoln the Orator*, 38.

40. Wolf, *Lincoln's Religion*, 181.

41. Paludan, *Presidency of Abraham Lincoln*, 305.

42. Wills, "Lincoln's Greatest Speech?" 70.

43. Frederick Douglass, *The Life and Times of Frederick Douglass, Written By Himself* (1892; reprint, New York: Collier Books, 1962), 366, 363.

44. Wills, "Lincoln's Greatest Speech?" 70.

45. Barondess, *Three Lincoln Masterpieces*, 81–83.

46. Ibid., 75.

47. Kazin, *God and the American Writer*, 120.

48. Wolf, *Lincoln's Religion*, 181.

49. Trueblood, *Abraham Lincoln*, 135.

50. Miller, "Lincoln's Second Inaugural," 53.

51. Donald, *Lincoln*, 566; Einhorn, *Abraham Lincoln the Orator*, 87.

52. Hawthorne, *Scarlet Letter*, 173.

53. Ibid., 176.

54. White, "Lincoln's Sermon on the Mount," 209.

EPILOGUE

1. Donald, *Lincoln*, 332.
2. Paludan, *Presidency of Abraham Lincoln*, 308.
3. Brodie, "Who Defends the Abolitionist?" 64.
4. Oates, *Abraham Lincoln*, 143.
5. McPherson, *Battle Cry of Freedom*, 852.
6. Donald, *Lincoln*, 583.
7. Fehrenbacher, *Lincoln in Text and Context*, 112.
8. Bennett, "Was Lincoln a White Supremacist?" 42.
9. Paludan, *Presidency of Abraham Lincoln*, 309.
10. Cox, *Lincoln and Black Freedom*, 142.
11. Oates, *Abraham Lincoln*, 144.
12. Roger Kahn, *The Boys of Summer* (New York: New American Library, 1971), xv–xvi.
13. Ibid., xvi. Significantly, Jackie Robinson broke baseball's color line after another great war. The Dodgers signed him to a minor league contract in August 1945, right after World War II ended. The United States had just fought a war to defeat the racist regime of Adolf Hitler, and many Americans began to cast a critical eye upon their own nation's racist policies. That Robinson was an army veteran probably helped his cause.
14. Oates, *Abraham Lincoln*, 144.
15. Current, *Lincoln Nobody Knows*, 234.
16. Douglass, *Life and Times*, 359.
17. Donald, *Lincoln*, 541.
18. Elizabeth Keckley, *Behind the Scenes: Or, Thirty Years a Slave, and Four Years in the White House* (New York: Oxford University Press, 1988), 156.
19. Wills, "Lincoln's Greatest Speech?" 70.
20. Hofstadter, *American Political Tradition*, 129.
21. Guelzo, *Abraham Lincoln*, 458.
22. Niebuhr, "Religion of Abraham Lincoln," 77.

INDEX